ENDPAPER

The *Stars and Stripes,* Richard Byrd's orange-winged Fairchild, takes off over the Bay of Whales in artist Paul Lengellé's conception of the explorer's first Antarctic flight on January 15, 1929. Fur-clad crew members on the ground pause during the unloading of supplies from the three-masted ship *City of New York* to wave encouragement as Byrd begins the one-and-a-half-hour flight. The orange flag at right marks the trail leading to Little America, Byrd's famous base eight miles away. This watercolor was created expressly for *The Explorers.*

THE EXPLORERS

Other Publications:
THE CIVIL WAR
PLANET EARTH
COLLECTOR'S LIBRARY OF THE CIVIL WAR
LIBRARY OF HEALTH
CLASSICS OF THE OLD WEST
THE GOOD COOK
THE SEAFARERS
THE ENCYCLOPEDIA OF COLLECTIBLES
THE GREAT CITIES
WORLD WAR II
HOME REPAIR AND IMPROVEMENT
THE WORLD'S WILD PLACES
THE TIME-LIFE LIBRARY OF BOATING
HUMAN BEHAVIOR
THE ART OF SEWING
THE OLD WEST
THE EMERGENCE OF MAN
THE AMERICAN WILDERNESS
THE TIME-LIFE ENCYCLOPEDIA OF GARDENING
LIFE LIBRARY OF PHOTOGRAPHY
THIS FABULOUS CENTURY
FOODS OF THE WORLD
TIME-LIFE LIBRARY OF AMERICA
TIME-LIFE LIBRARY OF ART
GREAT AGES OF MAN
LIFE SCIENCE LIBRARY
THE LIFE HISTORY OF THE UNITED STATES
TIME READING PROGRAM
LIFE NATURE LIBRARY
LIFE WORLD LIBRARY

FAMILY LIBRARY:
HOW THINGS WORK IN YOUR HOME
THE TIME-LIFE BOOK OF THE FAMILY CAR
THE TIME-LIFE FAMILY LEGAL GUIDE
THE TIME-LIFE BOOK OF FAMILY FINANCE

*This volume is one of a series that traces the adventure and
science of aviation, from the earliest manned balloon ascension
through the era of jet flight.*

THE EXPLORERS

by Donald Dale Jackson

AND THE EDITORS OF TIME-LIFE BOOKS

TIME-LIFE BOOKS, ALEXANDRIA, VIRGINIA

Time-Life Books Inc.
is a wholly owned subsidiary of

TIME INCORPORATED

FOUNDER: Henry R. Luce 1898-1967

Editor-in-Chief: Henry Anatole Grunwald
President: J. Richard Munro
Chairman of the Board: Ralph P. Davidson
Executive Vice President: Clifford J. Grum
Editorial Director: Ralph Graves
Group Vice President, Books: Joan D. Manley
Vice Chairman: Arthur Temple

TIME-LIFE BOOKS INC.

EDITOR: George Constable
Executive Editor: George Daniels
Director of Design: Louis Klein
Board of Editors: Dale M. Brown, Thomas A. Lewis,
Martin Mann, Robert G. Mason, John Paul Porter,
Gerry Schremp, Gerald Simons, Rosalind Stubenberg,
Kit van Tulleken
Director of Administration: David L. Harrison
Director of Research: Carolyn L. Sackett
Director of Photography: John Conrad Weiser

PRESIDENT: Reginald K. Brack Jr.
Executive Vice Presidents: John Steven Maxwell,
David J. Walsh
Vice Presidents: George Artandi, Stephen L. Bair,
Peter G. Barnes, Nicholas Benton, John L. Canova,
Beatrice T. Dobie, James L. Mercer, Paul R. Stewart

THE EPIC OF FLIGHT

EDITOR: Dale M. Brown
Designers: Van W. Carney, Albert Sherman
Chief Researcher: W. Mark Hamilton

Editorial Staff for *The Explorers*
Associate Editors: Jim Hicks, Ellen Phillips (text);
Jane N. Coughran (pictures)
Staff Writers: Rachel Cox, Allan Fallow, Adrianne Goodman,
Glenn Martin McNatt, Robert Menaker
Researchers: Marguerite Johnson, M. Linda Lee,
Gregory McGruder, Jules Taylor
Assistant Designer: Anne K. DuVivier
Copy Coordinators: Stephen G. Hyslop, Anthony K. Pordes
Picture Coordinators: Betsy Donahue, Renée DeSandies
Editorial Assistant: Constance B. Strawbridge

Editorial Operations
Design: Arnold C. Holeywell (assistant director);
Anne B. Landry (art coordinator); James J. Cox
(quality control)
Research: Jane Edwin (assistant director), Louise D. Forstall
Copy Room: Susan Galloway Goldberg (director),
Celia Beattie
Production: Feliciano Madrid (director), Gordon E. Buck,
Peter A. Inchauteguiz

Correspondents: Elisabeth Kraemer (Bonn); Margot
Hapgood, Dorothy Bacon (London); Miriam Hsia, Lucy T.
Voulgaris (New York); Maria Vincenza Aloisi, Josephine du
Brusle (Paris); Ann Natanson (Rome). Valuable assistance
was also provided by: Helga Kohl (Bonn); Robert Kroon
(Geneva); Lesley Coleman (London); Felix Rosenthal
(Moscow); Christina Lieberman (New York); Dag
Christensen (Oslo); Mimi Murphy, Ann Wise (Rome).

THE AUTHOR

Donald Dale Jackson, a former staff writer for *Life,* is the author of several Time-Life books, including *Underground Worlds* in the Planet Earth series, *Sagebrush Country* in the American Wilderness series, and *The Aeronauts* and *Flying the Mail* for The Epic of Flight. He spent a year at Harvard University as a Nieman Fellow. Among his other books are *Judges,* a history of the United States judicial system, and *Gold Dust,* a narrative history of the California gold rush.

THE CONSULTANTS

Richard K. Smith, the principal consultant, is a former historian at the National Air and Space Museum in Washington, D.C. He is the author of several aeronautical histories, including *First Cross! The U.S. Navy's Transatlantic Flight of 1919,* which was awarded the 1972 history prize of the American Institute of Aeronautics and Astronautics. He also serves as American literary editor of the British aviation monthly *Air International* and teaches a course on the history of mechanical flight at the University of Maryland.

Dana Bell, a staff member of the National Air and Space Museum, has done extensive research on the history of color schemes in military and commercial aircraft. He is the author of several books, including *Air Force Colors,* a two-volume history of U.S. Air Force aircraft camouflage.

For information about any Time-Life book, please write:
Reader Information
Time-Life Books
541 North Fairbanks Court
Chicago, Illinois 60611

Library of Congress Cataloguing in Publication Data
Jackson, Donald Dale, 1935-
    The explorers.
    (The Epic of flight)
    Bibliography: p.
    Includes index.
    1. Aeronautics—Flights. 2. Exploration.
3. Polar regions—Aerial exploration. I. Time-Life Books
II. Title.   Series.
TL721.1.J33   910.4   82-19551
ISBN 0-8094-3366-4
ISBN 0-8094-3367-2 (lib. bdg.)

CONTENTS

Conquerors of the world's last frontiers

One day in 1892, when Lincoln Ellsworth was 12 years old, he looked through his father's oversized atlas and became intrigued by the blank spaces marked "Unexplored" that capped both ends of the earth and dotted several continents. "Why don't people go there?" he wondered. "What can be in those white places?"

In the early years of the century and right up to World War II, a handful of brave men and women went in search of the answers. Among them was Ellsworth, who won renown as a polar explorer. These pioneers were aided in their quest by the development of long-range aircraft that enabled them not only to vault the barriers that had held others back but to see in hours what would have taken days, weeks and even years of patient slogging by any other means. "Discoveries leap upon the aerial adventurer down here," said Richard E. Byrd of his first flights across Antarctica in 1928. And in 1929, the Australian explorer George Hubert Wilkins exulted: "We covered 1,200 miles in a straight line in the Arctic that had never been seen by man last year. We added another 1,200 miles to the map in Antarctica last December. This year we hope, by flying from the Ross Sea, south of New Zealand, to add another 2,000 miles of coastline to the map."

Even the veteran explorer Roald Amundsen, whose early expeditions to the Arctic and Antarctic had been by ship and dog team, had to admit that such once-esteemed methods of exploration were outmoded. "Their place now," he wrote, "though forever glorious, is in the museum and the history books. The future of exploration lies in the air."

But while planes may have made it possible to visit hitherto unreachable places, the explorers, just like those in ages past, had still to be willing to risk their lives, as well as their life savings and the investments of trusting backers. But all found the risks, carefully weighed, worth taking. "No matter how hazardous an endeavor might be," wrote Byrd, "it is justifiable when the end sought is human knowledge." Pilot Bernt Balchen, who accompanied Byrd on the 1929 flight to the South Pole, felt that another motive might be involved. "What driving force," he asked, "causes a man to leave comfort and security, and risk hunger and privation and even death in search of something he cannot keep even when he finds it?"

Whatever that force was, whether ambition, intellectual curiosity or financial gain—or a combination of factors—the supreme triumph for these indomitable aviators, whose portraits appear on the following pages, was a deep feeling of accomplishment. Wrote Amundsen: "Whatever remains to man unknown in this world of ours remains a continuing evidence of man's weakness. But every mystery made plain, every unknown land explored, exalts the spirit of the whole human race—permanently."

ROALD AMUNDSEN
Norway's Roald Amundsen was described by a journalist as having "the eyes of a man who had looked over great open spaces all his life." Despite an austere countenance, he had great warmth and humor. "Underneath," wrote the reporter, "there still lingered much of the spirit of a boy."

BERNT BALCHEN

"Life for me is always adventure after adventure," said Byrd's South Pole pilot. Norwegian-born Balchen had applied for U.S. citizenship, but he violated the residency requirement by going to Antarctica and was threatened with deportation upon his return. Congress responded by making him a citizen.

ALAN COBHAM

Alan Cobham, shown with the movie camera used on his 1925 survey flight from London to South Africa, filmed his aerial adventures "so that the British public might share all our experiences." From 1923 to 1931, Cobham pioneered air routes in Africa, Australia, Asia and Europe.

RICHARD E. BYRD

Byrd developed an early taste for exploration when at the age of 12, with his parents' blessing, he went off alone to visit a friend in the Philippines. "Go where he may," his Naval Academy yearbook said of the midshipman, "he cannot hope to find the truth, the beauty, pictured in his mind."

WOLFGANG VON GRONAU

Director of a marine flight training school in Germany, Gronau made three trailblazing flights from Europe to the United States via the Arctic in 1930, 1931 and 1932. Upon completing the first of these, the former World War I pilot said, "One must have some daring if one is to live one's dreams. So I just went."

MARTIN AND OSA JOHNSON

After meeting at a nickelodeon Martin Johnson operated in Kansas, the Johnsons eloped and two years later left on the first of their many journeys to the world's wild places. Both learned to fly in 1932, and their books and movies about their African adventures became favorites of American audiences.

LINCOLN ELLSWORTH

To prepare for a life "devoted to solitude and physical hardship," Ellsworth spent 25 years traveling and studying before beginning his famous polar explorations. He financed most of his own expeditions, and in 1935 and 1939 he claimed 430,000 square miles of Antarctica for the United States.

ANNE AND CHARLES LINDBERGH

"In order to be alone, we had to fly," said Anne Lindbergh, whose famed husband, Charles, attracted crowds everywhere. Together, they flew survey flights to the Orient and Europe, scouting out new Arctic air routes. "It wasn't a settled life," she wrote. "We just lived in the plane, really, at the beginning."

WALTER MITTELHOLZER

A crash during a solo flight across the Alps in 1922 nearly ended Mittelholzer's flying career before it was fairly begun. Cured of what he called "my impetuous foolhardiness," the Swiss pilot—who was also an aerial photographer—became renowned for his exploratory flights in Africa and the Arctic.

GEORGE HUBERT WILKINS

At the age of 20, Australian George Hubert Wilkins decided to "stow away on a ship without knowing where it was going," and thus began 50 years of journeys into the unknown. Though he learned to fly in 1909, the self-educated explorer disliked exams and refused at the time to test for his pilot's license.

FLOYD BENNETT

Chosen by Byrd to pilot the first flight to the North Pole in 1928, Navy man Bennett became a hero to the public. When he died two years later of pneumonia, at 38, thousands lined streets in New York and Washington to see his cortege go by. He was buried in Arlington Cemetery, with honors accorded an admiral.

1

The race to the top of the world

The dream of the explorer is as old as the dream of flight itself. For countless centuries, the urge to cross uncharted seas and stand on mysterious shores inspired men to leave home and safety and to venture the unknown—on foot, on horseback, in ships and then, in the early years of this century, in aircraft, invented, it seemed, especially for explorers. A flier—and at the end of World War I there were plenty of trained pilots looking for new challenges—could reach places so forbidding that on the map of the globe they still were marked "Unexplored." The ice-locked wildernesses of the Arctic and Antarctic, barely penetrated by adventurers on foot and in ships, remained enigmas, as did the myriad islands that dotted the far Pacific. The dense interiors of Africa and South America were no more than featureless jungle, and there existed not a single reliable guide to the highest mountain chain in the world, the Himalayas.

Among the company of bold and restless aviators who responded to this challenge were America's Richard Byrd, the great Australian explorer George Hubert Wilkins and Norway's Roald Amundsen, all of whom earned glory at the Poles. An American, Richard Archbold, was one of those who explored in the Pacific; he discovered a valley in New Guinea inhabited by a people unknown to the world outside. A Briton, Alan Cobham; a Swiss, Walter Mittelholzer; and the American couples Martin and Osa Johnson, and Richard and Mary Light all helped open Africa to fliers. Charting the Himalayas was a British team, led by Peregrine Fellowes. Following close on the heels of the explorers came trailblazers such as Charles and Anne Lindbergh, their fellow Americans Bert Hassell and Parker Cramer, Germany's Wolfgang von Gronau and the Soviet Union's Valery Chkalov. Under circumstances only slightly less hazardous and uncertain than those faced by those who had flown ahead of them, these aviators charted air routes that would one day open the world's remote places to the everyday traveler. To the public, excitedly following these exploits from the sidelines, the fliers seemed to be living one of the great adventures of the age.

The first challenge to the new explorers was the Arctic and its immense frozen ocean, encompassing an area twice the size of the United

Embarking on their quest for the North Pole, 760 miles distant, the American explorers Richard Byrd and Floyd Bennett bank their Fokker over the snowy landscape of Spitsbergen on May 9, 1926.

States and stretching across the top of the world from Alaska to Siberia and northern Europe. Only a fraction of the Arctic had been explored at all. Only one man, the American Robert E. Peary, had reached lat. 90° N.—the North Pole. That was in 1909 and Peary had used dog sleds and his own two feet for the epic journey. There remained more than a million square miles of ice-covered realm to explore. No one knew how deep the ocean was or whether land, which Peary thought he saw, and which he named Crocker Land after one of his patrons, actually existed. But everyone was curious—especially about land. Perhaps a whole continent waited beyond the Arctic Circle.

The idea of exploring the Arctic by air was not a new one. The first balloon flights in the late 18th Century had inspired Thomas Jefferson to predict that balloons would lead to the discovery of the Poles. A century later, in 1897, a Swedish engineer named Salomon Andrée actually tried to fly across the North Pole in a balloon. But balloons remained stubbornly wedded to the wind, resisting all attempts to make them maneuverable. Andrée's balloon went down three days after its ascent from the Norwegian island of Spitsbergen, and his remains were not found until 1930. Airships—huge streamlined balloons powered by engines and steered with rudders—had not yet evolved into practical vehicles for exploration in 1909, when Walter Wellman, an American journalist, tried to navigate the Arctic in an early model. Bad weather had defeated a previous attempt and the failure of the airship's untried ballast equipment defeated this one; Wellman gave up.

Balloons would not do and airships appeared to be too fragile. But airplanes—faster and sturdier than any lighter-than-air craft—seemed to hold the answer. Peary himself noted in 1920 that planes could survey in weeks an area that took years for a ground party to cover.

The difficulties remained formidable. No aviators anywhere had confronted the forbidding range of obstacles to flying that the North presented. Storms broke virtually without warning and persisted for weeks. The forces emanating from the Magnetic North Pole, located at the fringe of the Arctic Circle, confounded conventional compasses. And the glaring endless light of summer, the only season when flying was feasible, made it difficult to detect a horizon and could blind a man in hours. In the altogether likely event of a forced descent away from land, pilots could expect only shifting pack ice that could open and close in seconds, plunging both aircraft and flier into the deadly sea.

It was not surprising, then, that the few flights made before 1920 had merely scratched at the Arctic's icy door. A Russian had flown 55 miles over the Barents Sea in a floatplane; Danish aviators had scouted Icelandic flying conditions; and four U.S. Army airmen had crossed Alaska from the Yukon to Nome. No one had flown over the Pole; and some thought a flight across the Arctic Ocean impossible. By 1920, however, pilots were ready to challenge the Far North. In the decade that followed, four brave men—Roald Amundsen, Lincoln Ellsworth, Richard Byrd and Hubert Wilkins—would lead attempts to conquer the Arctic.

Amundsen, at 54, was the oldest and toughest of them all. In 1911, the famed explorer became the first man to reach the South Pole on foot. He also was the first to navigate the long-sought Northwest Passage, in 1906, threading his small sailing ship among the Arctic islands of Canada between the Atlantic and Pacific Oceans. The trip convinced him that the way to explore the Poles was by air, and to this end he obtained the first Norwegian pilot's license in 1912. Sure that he could fly across the Arctic Ocean, from Alaska to Europe, the "Old Viking," as he was called, bought a Farman biplane in 1914. World War I forced him to abandon his plan, but in 1922 Amundsen headed for Alaska with a long-range Junkers J-13 monoplane fitted with skis. Unfortunately, the plane was damaged beyond immediate repair in test flights, the Arctic winter began to close in, and the expedition was scuttled.

Undaunted, Amundsen returned to Norway to engage in the explorer's perennial quest for financial backing. Outfitting a polar expedition with planes, crews and provisions, and chartering ships to transport them all, could cost hundreds of thousands of dollars that had to be raised piecemeal—from private patrons, scientific organizations and newspapers in search of dramatic stories. Despite his enormous reputation in his homeland, Amundsen could find no Norwegian backers for a polar exploration as dubious as one employing an airplane. On top of that, his personal money problems were particularly acute. The man who handled his finances during his long absences had succeeded in bankrupting the explorer painfully and publicly.

Desperate for funds and hounded by creditors, Amundsen journeyed to the United States in 1924 to raise money by writing and lecturing, but with little success. Eventually, in October of that year, after a disheartening swing around the lecture circuit, he found himself alone in a New York hotel room, brooding that a glorious career had come to an inglorious end. Then the telephone rang.

The caller introduced himself as Lincoln Ellsworth and asked to come up and talk. Amundsen—scornful of time-wasting discussions with hero worshippers (and wary of process servers)—was about to dismiss the man when Ellsworth mentioned that he might be able to supply money for an Arctic expedition. Amundsen immediately invited him to his room—and thus began a famous and successful partnership.

Ellsworth, at 44, felt as if he had spent his life preparing for this meeting. The son of a wealthy businessman, he had been a timid and sickly child, and he had something to prove. "I delighted to match my powers against hardships under which men of lesser strength wilted," he later wrote. Trained as an engineer, he had roughed it as a railroad worker in the Canadian West and learned to fly in France during World War I. He had only recently returned from leading an expedition across the Andes, and a trip to Peru was in the offing. But exploring the Arctic with the master—Roald Amundsen—was Ellsworth's dream.

The plain-speaking, matter-of-fact Amundsen and the courtly, deferential Ellsworth spent that evening excitedly discussing a new aerial assault on the Arctic. Their goal was to learn whether a continent did indeed lie hidden somewhere in the Far North by flying across the Arctic Ocean from the Norwegian island of Spitsbergen to the northern coast of Alaska. The distance—if they flew across the Pole— would be 1,700 miles.

No plane suitable for Arctic conditions had a range that great. But Amundsen had a scheme, and he became animated as they talked. His idea was to use two aircraft. He knew he could get planes that carried almost enough fuel for the transarctic trip, and these would fly to the Pole and land. One plane would be abandoned after its fuel was transferred to the other, thus extending the second craft's range. That plane, with the entire team aboard, would fly on to Alaska. To ease the anxieties of their backers, the explorers would announce only that they were making an aerial dash from Spitsbergen to the Pole and back, a feat within the capabilities of several of the era's longest-ranged aircraft.

What was needed first, of course, was money. While Ellsworth was the son of a multimillionaire, he was not personally wealthy and had to persuade his father to contribute $85,000. This would cover the bulk of the expedition's cost and encourage other potential backers, including the Aero Club of Norway, to put up the remaining funds. This proved a difficult task, for the old man was certain that he was sending his only son to his death. Ellsworth finally prevailed, and cash in hand, he and Amundsen began preparing for their great adventure.

The explorers needed crack crews and the best possible aircraft. For pilots, Amundsen selected Norway's two top aviators, Hjalmar Riiser-Larsen and Lief Dietrichson. The pilots in turn chose the planes—two German-designed Dornier-Wal (whale, in German) twin-engined flying boats with sturdy aluminum hulls that permitted takeoffs not only from water, but when conditions were right, from ice as well. Each Dornier-Wal could carry six people and had a range of 1,500 miles, only slightly less than the distance from Spitsbergen to Alaska.

Amundsen and Ellsworth worked fast. They wanted to make the expedition in 1925, and it had to be planned for the four months between April and September. Only then did sinuous cracks called leads open in the jumbled wilderness of ice, exposing enough water for flying-boat landings and takeoffs.

By May of 1925, the expedition was well established in the tiny coal-mining town of Kings Bay, Spitsbergen. It was the closest jumping-off point to the North Pole, 760 miles distant. The planes, which had arrived by ship, were assembled and overloaded—by 1,000 pounds each—with supplies, including fuel, cameras and, in case of a forced landing, sleds, tents, canvas boats, skis and a month's rations.

But the most critical equipment was that needed for navigation, and Amundsen saw to it that his men had the best then available, though even this was not entirely trustworthy. Their standard magnetic compasses probably would function erratically so near the Magnetic Pole; their sextants, whose measurements depended on fixing points in rela-

A journalist's polar folly

Once New York journalist Walter Wellman made up his mind to become the first man to reach the North Pole, there was no stopping him. Despite the danger, he set off on August 15, 1909, from Danes Island, Spitsbergen, in the *America*, a 10-ton, hydrogen-filled dirigible. All his hopes rested on his propeller-driven airship, which he saw as "big and stout, steel-muscled, full-lunged, built for work, for endurance, able to fight the winds that sentry the Pole and perhaps to defeat them."

Wellman had equipped the *America* with two 130-foot-long leather tubes, six inches in diameter, covered with small steel plates and stuffed with emergency food and supplies. One, known as the equilibrator, was to function as ballast and guide rope. With its end snaking along the ice and snow, it would keep the airship, as Wellman put it, "in continuous contact with *terra firma*." The other tube, called the retarder, was barbed to act as a kind of drag anchor that could be thrown overboard to slow the ship.

All went smoothly for 32 miles. Then without warning the 1,200-pound equilibrator broke loose, and the unburdened airship shot straight up. Wellman's three-man crew, ears ringing from the ascent, managed to get the *America* under control by letting out hydrogen and headed it back toward Danes Island. After spotting a steamer below, they threw a line to her, boarded her, and the ship towed the dirigible the rest of the way.

Wellman's hard luck was not yet over. When his crew tried to secure the *America* to shore, the airship escaped. Buoyed by gusts, it rose 6,000 feet and exploded. The final blow, however, came when the would-be explorer learned that even before he left the United States for Spitsbergen Admiral Peary had reached the Pole. "How much trouble I would have saved," he later wrote, "if I had known."

Walter Wellman leans resolutely on the railing of the deck of the America, the 185-foot-long dirigible in which he hoped to become the first to conquer the North Pole.

After rising out of control, the America is brought down to the sea and maneuvered into position so the men and 10 sled dogs aboard can be transferred to the rescue ship.

tion to the horizon, would be more accurate at sea level than in a moving plane; and their most advanced device, a sun compass, required a clear sky to be effective. This instrument operated like a sundial in reverse. With a sundial, direction is known, and the shadow of the sun falling on the dial's face indicates the time; with a sun compass, the time is known and the shadow on the compass face indicates direction.

The explorers had now only to wait for a break in the always unpredictable weather of the springtime Arctic, and the break came on May 21. At 5 p.m. the two aircraft, known simply as the *N-24* and the *N-25,* revved up for takeoff from the ice that covered Kings Bay harbor. As the planes gathered speed the ice seemed about to buckle under their weight; then they bumped into the air and rose into the northern sky. In the forward observation seat of the *N-25's* open cockpit sat Amundsen; Riiser-Larsen, the pilot, sat behind him, and a German employee of Dornier named Karl Feucht occupied the mechanic's station near the 365-horsepower Rolls-Royce Eagle IX engines. Lief Dietrichson was at the controls of the *N-24,* with Ellsworth as navigator and a Norwegian named Oskar Omdal as mechanic.

Soon the fur-clad adventurers were winging above a light fog, straining for a glimpse of whatever lay beneath it. From his perspective in the *N-24's* nose, Ellsworth gazed down and "felt like a god." Beneath each plane traveled perfect double circles of rainbow, caused by refracted light bouncing off water droplets, and in the center of the rings sped the sharp shadows of the planes, flying abreast so that the men could communicate with one another by hand signals. Radios ordered for the flight had not arrived in time.

After two hours, the fog began to tatter, then abruptly the aircraft cleared the fog bank. Ellsworth, crouching behind his windshield to avoid the knifelike cold, saw stretched beneath him the "great frozen North itself." He estimated that each hour of flight brought into view more than 9,000 square miles of territory never before seen.

Pilot Dietrichson was less awed by the terrain, having other matters to consider. Where could he land if he had to? No aviator had ever hunted for an answer in a world like this; he could see no possibilities, nothing—just narrow, twisting dark leads and expanses of ice covered by mounds and ridges.

The explorers had been airborne for just under eight hours when they sighted a lead wide enough to land in. Half their fuel was gone and Amundsen was anxious to calculate their precise position from the vantage point of the sea below: During the hours of flying in fog, he could not use the sun compass, and in addition, the plane's motion made accurate sextant readings difficult. Amundsen had had to depend on dead reckoning for navigation, calculating position by keeping a record of the distance the plane had traveled along the course he had set from Spitsbergen. But for accurate dead reckoning, Amundsen needed to know how far crosswinds were pushing the plane off course, and during foggy periods, there was no way to determine this. He estimated,

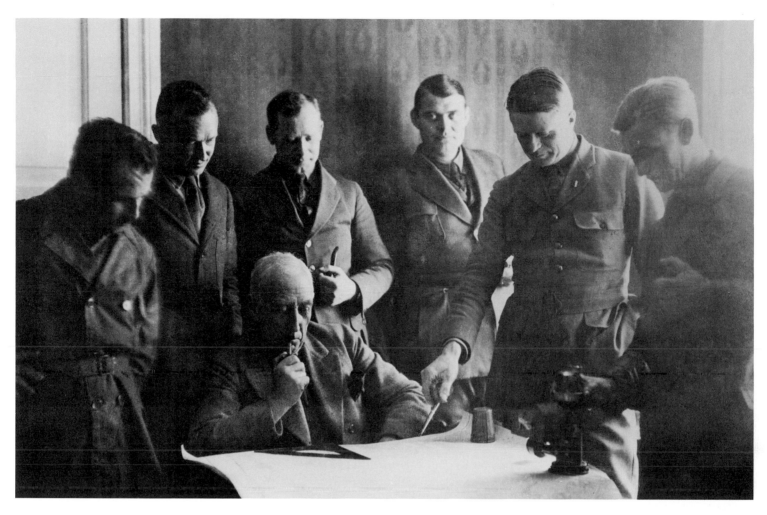

Explorers Roald Amundsen (seated) and Lincoln Ellsworth (second from left) go over their projected route with their flight crews on the eve of their 1925 attempt to reach the North Pole in two seaplanes.

however, that the expedition was nearing the Pole, and signaled for Riiser-Larsen to set the plane down in the lead.

As they descended, the men got a closer view of the awesome world that awaited them—upended ice blocks, gulchlike leads, pressure ridges (great walls of ice thrust up by wind and water currents) and bergs of old, blue Arctic ice 20 or 30 feet high. Without warning, one of the N-25's engines cut out. Now they had to come down. Unruffled, Riiser-Larsen expertly guided the N-25 between bergs and smacked it down in the slush-filled lead. One wing grazed a small berg before the plane came to rest with its nose buried in a pile of ice.

Dietrichson in the N-24 flew on until he spotted an ice-free lagoon three miles away. He landed smoothly on the water, the plane's nose coasting up onto an ice floe, but all was not well. "Omdal, Omdal," he shouted to the mechanic, "the plane is leaking like hell." Several rivets in the N-24's hull had been sheared, probably during takeoff from the ice on Kings Bay, and the plane was filling rapidly. If it sank, the fuel needed to get the expedition off the ice pack would go to the bottom.

Ellsworth and Dietrichson stepped onto the ice to assess the situation, and Omdal began pumping out the fuselage. An observation taken with the sextant fixed their position; it was, they found to their disgust, quite different from what they had expected. They were at lat. 87° 44', one hundred and fifty miles away from the Pole. Omdal examined the rear engine of the *N-24* and reported that it had been damaged in landing and its exhaust system had burned out. The *N-25* was nowhere in sight.

There followed a nightmare of effort lasting four days. Ellsworth, Dietrichson and Omdal had to get the *N-24* out of the water to prevent it from sinking or being crushed by the shifting ice. Somehow they had to repair the damaged engine. And if they were to survive, they would have to reunite with Amundsen and his crew. The three wrestled the *N-24* all the way onto the ice and pumped out the hull. Omdal set to work on the engine. Dietrichson and Ellsworth glimpsed the *N-25* far in the distance and began an exhausting series of attempts to reach their companions. But they were defeated each time by the deep drifts of snow and the fractured ice. Worse, Dietrichson, who had neglected to wear the goggles that would have protected his eyes against the retina-burning glare of the snow, was blinded within hours. He lay in the tent for a day, sleepless and with bandaged eyes. When his sight returned, he set out once more with Ellsworth. After seven hours of struggling across the snow and ice, they had gone only two miles and gave up.

What saved the expedition was the very thing that threatened it—the constant shift and drift of the ice floes, which carried the *N-24* steadily toward Amundsen and his party. By May 23—two days after the landing—the two groups were close enough to communicate with signal flags, a process that took hours, as none of the men were experts, and each signal had to be looked up in an instruction manual. By May 26, the gap between the planes had narrowed to a lead half a mile wide covered with thin young ice and towering hummocks of older ice.

Dietrichson and Ellsworth signaled to Amundsen that the *N-24* was not going to fly, despite all Omdal's work. There was no way the burned-out exhaust could be repaired, but that was a minor problem: The valves necessary for fuel compression functioned so poorly that the engine would not start. Amundsen, however, had good news: The *N-25* could fly. Ellsworth and his companions crammed food and supplies into backpacks and set out gingerly across the ice-covered lead that separated them from their comrades.

It was a nerve-shattering trip. The three men spread out, Ellsworth and Omdal going first to distribute their weight over the thin ice. Suddenly Dietrichson screamed and fell through. An instant later the ice gave way under Omdal. Amundsen, trapped helplessly out of sight behind an ice ridge at the far edge of the lead, felt his hair rise at the sound of the shout. He knew he could not reach the men. But Ellsworth crawled sideways onto a solid block until he reached a position where he could extend a ski to Dietrichson, who scrambled out of the water. Ellsworth then wriggled over to the nearly unconscious Omdal and grabbed his pack, holding on until Dietrichson helped him, and together they pulled Omdal to safety. The shivering men crawled from ice block to ice block until they reached Amundsen.

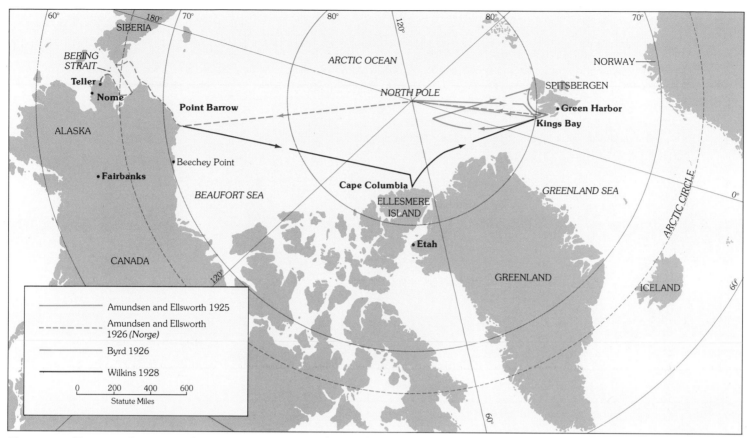

The routes of four expeditions over the Arctic between 1925 and 1928 are shown here. Failing to reach the North Pole from Spitsbergen by airplane in 1925, Roald Amundsen and Lincoln Ellsworth succeeded the following year in the dirigible Norge—but only after Richard Byrd had already flown there and back. Hubert Wilkins' 1928 flight from Point Barrow, Alaska, to Spitsbergen was the first eastward crossing of the Arctic Ocean.

Amundsen, Ellsworth thought, had aged 10 years in the few days they had been apart, but the old explorer was as cool and clearheaded as ever. He knew that haphazard living was the quickest way to break men under strain and he had organized his party for survival, with a regular schedule of work, meals and sleep. Food consisted primarily of hot chocolate and a stew made from water and pemmican, a dried mixture of powdered beef, vegetables and fat—with a ration of three quarters of a pound a day. Fresh water was no problem, even in the almost rainless environs of the North Pole: Sea ice loses its salinity after two or three years, and there was plenty of old sea ice to melt.

Though the N-25 was in flyable condition—the break in the air intake that had caused the engine failure had been repaired—the plane was precariously perched on a tongue of ice that projected into the now-frozen lead where Riiser-Larsen had landed. The task at hand was to get the craft to a safe place before the ice could crush it. The job had been too big for the three men in Amundsen's party, but six could do it. With the help of an anchor used as a pick, a small ax, shovels, and knives lashed to ski poles—the only digging tools that the otherwise well-equipped expedition carried—the men pried the plane free and slid it into a safe position on a large ice floe. The task took the entire day of May 27.

Now the problem was to get off the floe. The explorers agreed that they would have to make their move by June 15: Their rations could not last much past that date. With spring breakup at hand, the explorers

Amundsen and Ellsworth's men struggle to level a runway for their Dornier-Wal after engine failure forced it down 150 miles from the Pole.

decided that their best chance was to wait for a lead long enough for a launching: 1,500 feet was the minimum. In the meantime they occupied themselves with various chores. They took depth soundings through the ice, and when a drop in the temperature froze the lead between the two aircraft solidly enough, they carried the remaining fuel and supplies in a sled from the abandoned plane to the *N-25*.

The lead they were waiting for failed to appear. The wind blew steadily and bitterly from the south, squeezing the ice into a jumbled mass. The explorers now had two alternatives: They could look for a floe long enough and flat enough to use for a runway, or they could start on a probably hopeless trek toward Spitsbergen over the broken and perilous ice, which would become even more unstable and dangerous as the Arctic summer advanced. The pilots searched for a floe and on June 6 they found a suitable one—half a mile away, across a field split by narrow, watery leads and blocked by a pressure ridge 30 feet thick. Dragging the plane there was a formidable task for men who by now were half starved; rations had been reduced to half a pound a day each, less than Admiral Peary fed his dogs on his polar journeys. Nevertheless, the six explorers hacked their way through the ice barrier with their flimsy tools and constructed bridges of ice blocks, bound with snow, across the open leads. They hauled the plane— taxiing it under power whenever they could—to the takeoff site and

Exhausted by their 25-day ordeal on the ice, Amundsen (center) and Ellsworth (second from right) arrive with their men aboard the sealer Sjoliv at Kings Bay, Spitsbergen, on June 16, 1925. During the three days they spent on the boat they slept almost continuously, "only waking," said Amundsen, "to devour the delicious seal meat steaks and the eider duck omelets prepared for us."

The Norwegian Coast Guard ship Heimdal tows Amundsen and Ellsworth's downed plane through the Greenland Sea after the Sjoliv delivered the exhausted men to Kings Bay. The Sjoliv was unable to tow the craft the 100 miles back to base.

then spent a week shoveling and tramping down snow on the ice to make a firm runway. Amundsen later estimated that in all they had moved 300 tons of ice.

It was now June 14, one day before their escape deadline, when they would have either to fly out or chance the foot journey over the ice. The team prepared for takeoff. They tried that evening after the temperature dropped, but the runway was still mushy from the day's thaw and they were unable to get up enough speed to lift off. They moved the plane to a section of clear ice where the skis would not freeze fast and waited overnight, unloading everything they could spare, including cameras and rifles.

Early on the morning of June 15, when the slush had frozen, they tried again. This time Riiser-Larsen pushed the plane up to 62 miles an hour, and it lurched into the air, heading for Spitsbergen. Eight hours later, a jammed rudder forced the party down in the sea off the island's north coast. After taxiing through the waves to shore, they were spotted by a sealing ship, which took them to Kings Bay. There they found that rescue planes dispatched from Norway were getting ready to search for them. The search had only just been mounted, for Amundsen had warned that he might be out of touch for weeks.

The six men were gaunt and exhausted. Dietrichson had broken off five of his front teeth in his fall through the ice, and the mechanic Feucht was in a black depression that had enveloped him early in the ordeal. But they were alive. And while they had not reached the Pole, they had proved that a flight to it was at least possible and that a flying boat— given luck—could take off from polar ice.

Amundsen and Ellsworth immediately set about mounting another expedition. This time, they were determined to use an airship. Dirigible design had been steadily improved during World War I, and flights made across the Atlantic and across the United States in the early 1920s showed that the giant airships could travel far greater distances than any airplane then built.

But Amundsen and Ellsworth now had competition. An ambitious young American naval officer named Richard Evelyn Byrd was also convinced that the North Pole could be conquered by air, and he intended to be the conqueror.

The 36-year-old Byrd, a small, slight man who in his youth had trained himself to become a tough and accomplished athlete, was distinguished by his extraordinary determination. At the Naval Academy, he had injured his leg seriously while attempting a difficult gymnastic stunt. Then, as an ensign, he fell down a ship's open hatchway, injuring the leg again, and the permanent limp he thus acquired dimmed his prospects for a successful career at sea—the Navy required its seagoing officers to be in perfect physical condition. Byrd therefore retired—as a lieutenant junior grade—then managed not only to persuade the Navy to hire him as a retired officer on active duty, but also to wangle an appointment to its new aviation school at Pensacola, Florida. He became a skilled pilot and navigator.

Byrd's obsession with the Arctic matched Amundsen's. As a boy he had written in his diary that he meant to be the first man to the North Pole. Peary's 1909 expedition killed that dream, but not Byrd's desire to get there: He still could be the first to fly over the Pole.

In 1924 he managed to secure an assignment as navigator aboard an airship on an Arctic mission. But that expedition was scrapped before it properly started, because the airship used proved unreliable on preliminary tests. Then, in August 1925, two months after Amundsen and Ellsworth arrived back in Spitsbergen, Byrd accompanied explorer Donald MacMillan on a National Geographic Society expedition from Etah, an Eskimo settlement in northwest Greenland. The party was equipped with three Loening seaplanes borrowed from the U.S. armed forces, and the aim was to survey the Canadian islands northwest of Etah from the air with a view toward establishing an advance base for further exploration the following year. The attempt was abandoned after three weeks of weather so bad that flying was possible on only four days. Even so Byrd managed a sortie over the icecap that covered the interior of Greenland. He thus became the first person to look down on what was, as he put it, the "greatest iceberg factory in the world."

Plainly buoyed by this baptism in the Arctic, Byrd was eager to try

THE FIGHT FOR THE NORTH POLE
Lampooning the aerial competition to reach the North Pole, a July 1925 cartoon features an Eskimo directing air traffic over the Pole. "Discoverers, keep to the right, please," read the caption. The cartoonist apparently was unaware that penguins exist only in the Antarctic.

again. "Aviation will conquer the Arctic—and the Antarctic, too," he wrote confidently in *The National Geographic Magazine.* The difficulties and hazards of reaching the Poles, he said, only increased their lure.

The drive to reach the North Pole by air intensified in late 1925 and early 1926, and there began what the newspapers and most of the public—but not those involved—exuberantly called the "Race to the Pole." It moved toward a climax in April 1926 when two expeditions, one led by Amundsen and Ellsworth and one by Byrd, converged on Kings Bay, Spitsbergen.

Amundsen and Ellsworth arrived first by sea. For their transpolar attempt, they had purchased a 348-foot airship from the Italian government; it was powered by three 230-horsepower Maybach engines and had a range of 3,500 miles, 1,000 miles more than the distance from Kings Bay to Nome, Alaska, the expedition's planned terminus. To give it low fuel consumption the airship had been made as light as possible: Its gondola and control cars were so small that the crew barely fitted in, and the fuel supply was so limited that there was little margin for error in navigation. To protect them from the cold, the engines, oil tanks and gas-exhaust valves were fitted with felt shields. In Italy the airship had been christened the *Norge* (Norway) with great fanfare—Benito Mussolini made a speech at the ceremony. It would be piloted by its designer, Umberto Nobile, from Rome to Kings Bay and then across the Pole to Nome.

Amundsen and Ellsworth found the little community buried to the eaves in snow and the harbor a jumbled mass of ice, but their advance party had done its work well and their camp was in good shape. The airship's hangar and mooring masts were in place, sheds for supplies had been constructed and there was even a miniature railroad for transporting supplies from the wharf to the camp. Amundsen and Ellsworth settled in to await the arrival of their airship and of Byrd, whose ship, the *Chantier,* appeared at the edge of the harbor ice six days after their own arrival.

The adventurous and diplomatic Byrd had done an impressive job of mounting his expedition. He had persuaded such magnates as Edsel Ford, John D. Rockefeller Jr. and Vincent Astor to help finance a flight from Kings Bay to the Pole and back. Using their money, he had purchased a ski-equipped Fokker Trimotor with Wright Whirlwind engines and a 1,500-mile range—almost exactly the length of the round trip he planned. In honor of his chief patron's daughter, Byrd christened the Fokker the *Josephine Ford.* He also bought a small Curtiss Oriole to use for scouting and photography. He had leased the *Chantier* from the Federal War Shipping Board for the sum of one dollar a year and accepted the donation of a large part of his supplies. His 50 crew members were paid volunteers—Naval Reserve officers, West Point cadets, college boys and merchant sailors.

The ship's departure from the Brooklyn Navy Yard on April 5 was celebrated by a crowd of 2,000, including several disappointed young women whose offers to join the crew had been rejected. The festivities got off on a lighthearted note when a group of furiously strumming ukulele players turned up to serenade Richard Konter, a crew steward and the author of *Dick's Ukulele Guide.* When the din subsided, Byrd in his farewell speech emphasized that his main goal was not just to reach the Pole, but "to explore unexplored area and to discover new land if it is there." He expressed confidence that the conquest of the Arctic by multiengined planes would "give an impetus to commercial aviation." He acknowledged his competition but emphasized that the explorers not only wished each other well but would stand by to assist each other if the need should arise.

Amundsen, too, had emphasized that he was taking part in a scientific expedition, not a race; nevertheless, there was a certain amount of tension when the Byrd party arrived at Kings Bay. Byrd wanted to dock the *Chantier* so that he could unload the plane and supplies it carried, but the harbor's lone wharf was occupied by a Norwegian Coast Guard ship, the *Heimdal,* whose boiler was malfunctioning and whose captain was disinclined to move his vessel out into the choppy, ice-choked harbor. Byrd and his men then constructed a large raft out of planks laid across small boats, lowered the plane onto it, and maneuvered it among the ice blocks and through the howling winds to shore—a feat that earned a cheer from the watching Norwegian crew. He ferried ashore the Curtiss Oriole and his supplies in the same fashion. The men then set to work packing down the snow on the slope near the water's edge to make a runway, almost in the shadow of the huge, roofless hangar that awaited the *Norge,* still en route from Rome.

After this inauspicious beginning, however, the two parties maintained a correct cordiality through the storm-ridden days that followed as each expedition waited for the break in the weather that would make flying possible. Ellsworth and Amundsen had Byrd to dinner on their base ship; Byrd reciprocated on the *Chantier.* They helped each other prepare for the ordeal that lay ahead. Appalled, for instance, that Byrd's men lacked the snowshoes that might save them in case of a forced landing, Ellsworth and a companion lent their own and the Norwegian crew built the Americans a sled.

The waiting went on. Byrd's taciturn and skillful pilot, Floyd Bennett, a Navy aviation mechanic, test-flew the *Josephine Ford,* which after minor mishaps cruised for two hours with a lower fuel consumption than the men had expected. On May 2 the weather cleared and Amundsen radioed Nobile, who had been standing by with the *Norge* at Leningrad, to come to Spitsbergen, and Byrd's crew speeded up their preparations for the flight. The airship arrived early on May 7, and Nobile, anxious to get away before Byrd, told Amundsen he could be ready to leave in six hours. The weather forecasts from Alaska were not encouraging, however, and Amundsen preferred to wait.

In the end, it was Byrd and Floyd Bennett who started first. On the evening of the *Norge's* arrival, Byrd called on Amundsen and Ellsworth and told them he planned to fly to the Pole the next day. "That is all right with us," Amundsen replied stonily.

Byrd's crew had already begun the 14-hour job of loading and readying the Fokker for flight. The aircraft carried 615 gallons of fuel—420 gallons in its wing and fuselage tanks and the rest in five-gallon cans stored in the cabin—extending its range to almost 2,200 miles. In addition, the crew packed in a shortwave radio operated by a hand-cranked dynamo, 400 pounds of pemmican plus enough other food for 10 weeks, the sled, a rubber boat for crossing open leads, a tent, an ax, knives, a primus stove, a medical kit, smoke bombs for signaling, guns and ammunition.

Byrd and Bennett attempted to take off on May 8, but the overloaded plane could not achieve the speed it needed for flight and simply plowed into a soft snow bank at the end of the runway. The crew then removed every possible bit of excess weight. At 1:30 a.m. the next day, the *Josephine Ford* lumbered down Byrd's ice-covered runway and eased into the air. Amundsen and Ellsworth, asleep in their cottage, were awakened by the roar of the plane's engines and ran out in time to see the Fokker vanish over the cliffs that walled the north side of Kings Bay harbor. The Byrd expedition was on its way to the North Pole.

Bennett, at the controls in the *Josephine Ford's* cockpit, leveled the plane off at 2,000 feet and 90 miles an hour. Behind him in the unheated cabin, Byrd—wearing pants made of polar-bear skin and sealskin

Members of Richard Byrd's polar expedition gingerly guide a raft bearing the Josephine Ford through the ice of Kings Bay, Spitsbergen, in late April 1926. The party was forced to ferry the plane ashore when the Norwegian ship in the background refused to move from its berth—the only one in the harbor—thus preventing the ship that had brought the plane from docking.

His back to the camera, Roald Amundsen watches his rival return from the Pole on May 9, 1926. So many well-wishers rushed out to greet Byrd that his

mittens—worked hard and steadily at a battery of navigational devices, including a sun compass; a bubble sextant, which provided an artificial horizon for aerial navigation; and a drift indicator that, when lowered through a trap door in the belly of the plane, helped measure the winds that continually pushed the Fokker off course.

Byrd had plotted a flight straight north for the 760-mile trip. It was critically important not only that he keep the plane on course but also that he keep a meticulously detailed flight log. The log would be his only proof that the expedition had in fact reached the Pole. Every three or four minutes, Byrd took wind-drift measurements through the trap door, suffering a mild frostbite on his face and one hand. Between the measurements, he took sun shots with the sextant and checked the results with the compasses. Using hand signals—his voice could not be heard over the roar of the engines—he kept Bennett on course. These were, he later wrote, "the busiest and most concentrated moments of my life."

The air was relatively smooth and the weather remained clear. The *Josephine Ford* was performing well. From time to time, Byrd relieved Bennett at the controls so that the pilot could stretch his legs and top off the plane's fuel tanks. Together he and Bennett studied the white waste beneath them for signs of animals or indications of land, but there were none. "We felt no larger than a pinpoint and as lonely as the tomb," Byrd wrote later, "as remote and detached as a star."

The only mechanical trouble popped up as the *Josephine Ford* neared the Pole. The starboard engine began to leak oil. Bennett passed a note back to Byrd that said, "That motor will stop." Bennett thought that they should attempt a landing for repairs, but with the prize almost in sight—and the story of Amundsen's hellish experience on the ice the previous year fresh in his mind—Byrd elected to go on. He reasoned that they were safer aloft than on the ice as long as the engine continued to function. Perhaps the leak would stop. Both kept their eyes anxiously on the oil gauge, and eventually the leak did stop. Byrd and Bennett discovered later that it had been due to a loose rivet; it ceased when the oil dropped below the level of the rivet.

The *Josephine Ford* had been in the air for eight hours when Byrd's instruments indicated that the plane was over the Pole. It looked no different from the vista that they had been staring at all morning—"the same stretch of brilliant white, marked by ridges, hummocks and a few leads recently frozen, showing green against white," he wrote. Byrd tapped Bennett on the shoulder and the two men, the first to fly over the North Pole, shook hands matter-of-factly. Byrd rubbed his lucky coin—one that Peary had taken overland to the Pole. They made a wide sweep around the point they calculated to be the Pole, taking sextant readings for confirmation and shooting still photographs and movies. Then they turned and headed back to Spitsbergen, aided by a friendly tail wind that boosted their speed to more than 100 miles an hour.

The seven-hour flight back was so uneventful as to be anticlimactic. Byrd and Bennett, who had had almost no sleep in the preceding 48 hours, grew drowsy. They took turns at the controls, spelling each other as sleepiness overcame them. At 4:30 p.m., 15 hours after takeoff, the *Josephine Ford* soared in over Kings Bay, just as Amundsen and Ellsworth were sitting down to dinner.

The reception was tumultuous. Bennett circled the settlement while the whistle on the *Chantier* screeched and men from both expeditions' camps raced to the airstrip. One of the first to greet the explorers on landing was Amundsen, his eyes brimming with tears. The usually imperturbable Norwegian was so choked with emotion that he could not speak, but he embraced Byrd, who recognized the depth of Amundsen's feeling. "I saw then," Byrd said later, "the great man beneath the cloak that all great men wear."

As the band on the Norwegian ship played *The Star Spangled Banner,* Byrd's men hoisted their commander and his pilot onto their shoulders and marched into camp. Byrd and Bennett, exhausted, went to sleep at once, but the next night both parties joined for a dinner celebrating the American feat and the imminent departure of the Norwegian expedition. Byrd gave Amundsen one of his sun compasses for the *Norge,* and to Ellsworth he gave the polar-bear pants and sealskin mittens that he had worn to the Pole.

The *Norge* rose majestically into the air on the morning of May 11, its gondola crowded with the two explorers, the 14-man crew, supplies and Nobile's pet dog. Byrd and Bennett in the swifter *Josephine Ford*

The Norge hugs the coastline of Spitsbergen shortly after lifting off from Kings Bay on the morning of May 11, 1926. This photograph was shot from the cockpit of Byrd's skiplane, the Josephine Ford, whose wing tip appears at top. The plane escorted the airship for the first hour of its flight to the North Pole.

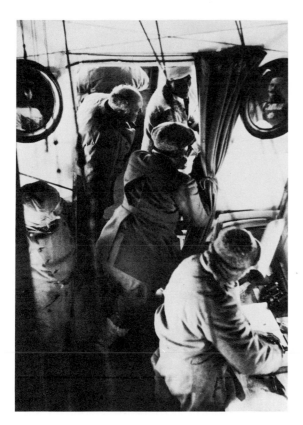

Standing in the gondola of the Norge, whose walls bear portraits of the Norwegian King and Queen, Amundsen's crew chart their progress over the top of the world. Most of the men stayed awake throughout the three-day journey because the cramped cabin offered no room to lie down.

gave escort for several miles, flying circles around the airship before departing with a farewell wave. They settled down to wait in Kings Bay: If the *Norge* ran into trouble, they would have to serve as a rescue team.

Radio bulletins arrived in Kings Bay from the *Norge* at regular intervals. Four hours after takeoff, the *Norge,* sailing along at 50 miles per hour, was at a latitude of 82° 30'; three hours later, it was at 85° N.; after another four and a half hours, the position was 88° N. The climactic bulletin came 15 hours after the airship had left Kings Bay: "North Pole, Wednesday, May 12—we reached the North Pole at 1 a.m. today and are now lowering flags for Amundsen, Ellsworth and Nobile." Two aerial expeditions had now reached the top of the world within four days.

A few hours later, as the *Norge* plunged into the unexplored region between the Pole and Alaska, the radio messages ominously stopped. No further word was heard for the next two days; ice had formed on the radio's transmitting antenna, preventing messages from getting out. The ship had even worse problems in the foul weather off the Alaskan coast. The fog was almost impenetrable, and Nobile was forced to change altitude repeatedly in an effort to get above or below it. Ice formed on the propellers, then flew off and bit holes in the craft's 348-foot-long fabric surface, and these had repeatedly to be repaired to protect the gas bags clustered inside the airship.

When the *Norge* reached Alaska, the weather had deteriorated even more and Nobile headed the dirigible out into the Bering Strait, where easterly winds threatened to blow it to Siberia. At last, 70 hours and 40 minutes after he had left Kings Bay and more than 50 hours since his final radio transmission, Nobile brought the *Norge* down in the tiny Alaskan coastal village of Teller, 3,180 miles from Spitsbergen. The second successful polar flight—the first transpolar flight—had come to an end.

The contenders in the polar race dispersed to collect their rewards and to describe their feats to the world. Amundsen, Ellsworth, Nobile and their crew sailed to Seattle, where they received a spectacular welcome. Byrd and his men in the *Chantier* steamed to London and then to New York for a hero's greeting on June 23, 1926. After a trip up Broadway amid a flurry of cheers and ticker tape, Byrd hurried to Washington to accept a gold medal from the National Geographic Society as well as the Congressional Medal of Honor, an award rarely given in peacetime.

Yet the explorers' great accomplishments were marred by controversy. The validity of Byrd's claim was challenged in several countries and still is. The argument was that he could not have made the polar flight in the 15 hours he took, given the *Josephine Ford's* average cruising speed of 90 miles an hour and the possibility that the tail winds Byrd claimed sped him home were nonexistent; weather charts for the day from Russia, Alaska and Spitsbergen all indicated calm air. Byrd's flight log and navigational computations, however, were examined and verified by National Geographic Society investigators. Amundsen and Nobile—who had been antagonistic from the beginning—engaged in a demeaning public quarrel about whether the Norwegian explorer or the Italian airman deserved credit for the success of the *Norge* expedition.

The drama eventually faded and the actors withdrew to the wings. Amundsen retired from exploration, leaving the field, he said, to younger men. Nobile returned to Italy, to contemplate further airship flights. Ellsworth went home to lead expeditions in search of fossil algae in the Grand Canyon and in the wilds of Labrador. Byrd set off to fly the Atlantic.

There still remained unanswered questions about the Arctic, however. Neither polar expedition had seen any land not already known to the cartographers, but the existence of land remained an intriguing possibility. That issue was to be settled once and for all by George Hubert Wilkins, who had been trying to reach the Pole for a year. Wilkins, in fact, had actually been in Alaska when the *Norge* arrived from the Pole, and had seen the airship floating overhead.

At the age of 37, Hubert Wilkins had logged enough adventures and engaged in enough professions to fill several volumes of biography. Brought up in the Australian Outback, he had studied both electrical and mechanical engineering in Adelaide while at the same time practicing the then-infant craft of film making. When he was 20, he stowed away on a ship bound for Africa. He eventually fetched up in England, where he worked as a news photographer, covering, among other events, the Balkan War of 1912. In 1913 he accompanied the Canadian polar explorer Vilhjalmur Stefansson as a photographer on Stefansson's expedition in the Beaufort Sea above Canada, a three-year exploration that taught Wilkins Eskimo techniques for Arctic survival. In World War I he served in the Royal Australian Flying Corps, and after the War he led a biological survey in remote northern Australia for the British Museum.

Wilkins' interest, however, centered on the Poles. He was convinced that chains of meteorological stations established in the polar regions could be used for accurate weather prediction, thereby lessening the effects of the terrible droughts he had seen in his Australian boyhood. The Stefansson expedition—and later, briefer excursions to the fringes of the Antarctic—had been his apprenticeship. Now he wanted to explore the Arctic, partly to see whether there was land suitable for meteorological stations and partly for the sheer joy of exploration, and he wanted to do it by airplane. His ultimate objective was a flight from Alaska to Spitsbergen.

Wilkins' experience as a newsman served him in good stead. The North American Newspaper Alliance, a syndicate, was looking for someone to fly in the Arctic—it was aware of the public's enthusiasm for stories of the mysterious North and its curiosity about a possible Arctic continent—and Stefansson himself had recommended the Australian. The syndicate, along with the Detroit Aviation Society and the *Detroit News,* sponsored an expedition in search of land, to be based in Alaska and commanded by Wilkins. It paid for the purchase and transportation of two Fokker airplanes, one a three-engined model similar to Byrd's and one with a single engine. It also paid for Wilkins' pilot, Carl Ben Eielson, a gifted 27-year-old American who had pioneered Alaskan bush flying and had become such a legend that the Indians of the Yukon called him "Brother to the Eagle."

Wilkins and Eielson arrived in Fairbanks in March of 1926, even as Amundsen and Byrd were approaching Spitsbergen to begin their polar flights. But no sooner had Wilkins and Eielson set up camp than disaster struck. A newspaperman was killed instantly when he walked into one of the moving propellers of the three-engined Fokker. Then the planes were taken up for test flights and both crashed on landing. Eielson and his backup pilot, Tom Lanphier, unfamiliar with the machines and the snow-covered runway, misjudged the approach on both occasions. Each throttled back too soon, causing the aircraft to stall and smash to the ground. Though Wilkins and Eielson managed an exploratory flight over the Arctic in the repaired single-engined Fokker, they were through exploring for that year—the larger plane could not be fixed before the flying season ended. The men spent the remainder of the spring ferrying fuel and supplies from Fairbanks to Point Barrow on Alaska's northern coast in preparation for another attempt the following year.

After crash-landing on its maiden flight in 1926, the Fokker Trimotor that Hubert Wilkins hoped to fly from Alaska to Spitsbergen lies crippled on a Fairbanks airfield. The plane skidded to a halt just yards from the spot where Wilkins and his pilot had wrecked their only other aircraft the day before.

In February 1927, Wilkins and Eielson established themselves at Point Barrow, determined to settle the question of whether any land existed between Alaska and the Pole. For this expedition the explorers had two single-engined Stinson Detroiter biplanes fitted with skis. Wilkins planned to use the planes, which had a range of 500 miles, for a series of flights over the Arctic. If no land was sighted, they would descend to the polar ice pack for another geographical task—taking soundings that would tell them the ocean's depth and reveal the formation of the continental shelf, which was believed to extend into the ocean from Siberia. Amundsen, whose own experiences on the polar ice convinced him that they would never find a floe large enough and flat enough for landing, thought the plan suicidal.

Wilkins and Eielson set out on March 29 in front of a blizzard that gave them a spanking tail wind, intending to fly a triangular course over the ocean for 14 hours. Trouble began 600 miles out when the Stinson's Whirlwind engine started misfiring. The explorers made an emergency landing on ice that happily turned out to be reasonably flat. Elated by this success, the incurably experimental Wilkins unloaded his sounding gear. While the plane's engine idled, he bored two holes in the ice, dangling a small microphone through one of them and dropping small explosive charges through the other; from the amount of time that elapsed between the dropping of each charge and the sound of its explosion on the ocean floor, he could calculate the depth of the water.

Presently Wilkins asked Eielson to switch off the engine so that he could hear the depth-charge echoes more clearly. Eielson, a man of few words, obeyed without comment, thinking to himself that if the engine were turned off for more than a few minutes he might not be able to restart it—the temperature on the ice was 30° below zero. In that event, no one but God and the two of them would know the results of the soundings. (They showed a depth of 16,000 feet, too much for the presence of a continental shelf.) The explorers worked on the Stinson's engine for two hours, starting it periodically to keep it warm. Eielson was forced to remove his gloves as he fiddled with the faulty ignition, and four fingers of his right hand were frostbitten in the icy blasts. When Wilkins later asked why his pilot had risked his fingers, Eielson replied that he preferred their loss to losing both arms and legs and what they were attached to.

At length the men were able to take off, only to be forced down again by their kicking, stalling engine after 10 minutes. They worked on the machine until they could leave the ice once more. But now a fierce head wind put a severe strain on their fuel supply. When the tank ran dry, Eielson crash-landed the plane on the ice, shearing off one wing. The explorers, uninjured, took their bearings—and discovered that they were on an ice floe 65 miles northwest of Point Barrow and drifting away from land. The two looked at each other and burst into a fit of nervous laughter.

They had no option now but to wait out the storm, which lasted four days, and to pick their way back across the ice floes to Point Barrow. They were fortunate in that they could shelter in the fuselage until the storm was over, and they had enough chocolate, biscuits, raisins, nuts and pemmican to last for several weeks. Wilkins, who knew how to keep warm and dry and how to build igloos to sleep in, could get them through the trek they had to make. On the fourth day Wilkins and Eielson started walking. When the ice sagged, they had to crawl. "A motion picture of our floundering," Wilkins wrote later, "would be considered much overacted." At one point Wilkins fell through and barely pulled himself out, then startled Eielson by stripping off his sealskin boots and rubbing them in the snow to dry them, all the while dancing maniacally to keep the blood flowing.

On April 15, almost two weeks after starting out, they reached the lonely trading post and radio station at Beechey Point, 300 miles east of Point Barrow, with no casualties other than one of Eielson's frostbitten fingers, which had to be amputated. Wilkins had not given up on his plan for a flight over the unexplored area from Alaska to Spitsbergen—but he would have to wait until his pilot was in condition and until he had a plane with sufficient range.

The solution to his problems literally came out of the blue. Recovering from his ordeal in San Francisco, Wilkins glanced out his hotel window one day and saw a clean-lined, swift-flying monoplane he called a bird of paradise. Wilkins traced the plane, which had been on its maiden flight, to an airfield in Oakland and learned from its designer that it was a Lockheed Vega, with a top speed of 135 miles an hour. The craft's range of 1,000 miles could be more than doubled by extra fuel tanks in the fuselage, just what Wilkins needed for the flight he planned. He immediately ordered a Vega for himself, paying for it by selling the trimotor Fokker, which had been stored in Seattle after his initial Arctic attempt. (The buyers, a pair of young Australians named Charles Kingsford-Smith and Charles Ulm, used the Fokker in 1928 to make the first flight across the Pacific, from Oakland, California, to Brisbane, Australia.)

Wilkins and Eielson flew the bright orange Vega, equipped this time with skis, to Point Barrow in March 1928. They were now ready for the transarctic journey. Wilkins, who would serve as navigator on the flight, had worked out a precise route. They would fly northeast from Point Barrow over the still-unknown portions of the Arctic, skirting the edge of Ellesmere Island, just west of Greenland; pass the northern tip of Greenland itself; and then cross to Spitsbergen, a trip of 2,200 miles halfway around the dome of the world. They were going to fly the polar ice, as Wilkins later put it, "in one big hop."

The aerial explorers began the trip in clear weather, with a mild head wind, on April 15, and the first few hours passed without mishap. The sun shone brightly, providing the men with unlimited visibility, but they saw no sign of land in the icy sea. The Vega passed through an extensive cloud system and then encountered a storm off Ellesmere Island. Eielson eased the plane down through it so that they could sight the island's glacial mountains, enabling Wilkins to confirm that they were on course. They passed Cape Columbia on Ellesmere Island, where Peary had begun his trek to the Pole 19 years before. They had now crossed the previously unexplored area of the Arctic. Wilkins sent a radio message to the president of the American Geographical Society, one of his sponsors. It said, "No foxes seen," a prearranged code (the society wanted the pleasure of announcing the news) that meant they had seen no land. The radio gave out soon afterward because of a failed generator.

Curving up the globe in their 16th hour of flight, the explorers crossed the tip of Greenland, but here their troubles began. A violent storm swirled beneath them and as they left it behind, Wilkins spotted in the distance the towering clouds that meant another storm awaited them. He passed a note to his pilot asking whether Eielson wanted to land on the smooth ice below to wait out the storm or take their chances on finding Spitsbergen. Eielson replied that as long as Wilkins could chart the course, he would fly it. They pushed on through the storm past the Greenland coast.

After two hours over the Greenland Sea, near Spitsbergen and with their goal almost in reach, they ran into yet another storm. Eielson dropped the shuddering, rocking plane lower and lower as they searched for land. At length they spotted a flat stretch of snow surrounded by the densely packed, heavily ridged ice that the Arctic-wise Wilkins knew meant land. With visibility near zero and fuel running low, they decided to make for it. In their descent they nearly collided with a mountain, but Eielson brought the plane down onto the snow patch with hardly a bump in the face of a gale so strong that the Vega came to a halt after rolling only 10 yards on the ground.

Wilkins and Eielson had been in the air for 20 hours and 20 minutes, making this the longest nonstop airplane flight yet carried out in the Arctic, and they had disposed of the land question completely. Their only problem was that while they knew they were on an island off Spitsbergen, they did not know exactly where it was. The storm was packing winds that registered 70 miles an hour on the Vega's wind-speed indicator, and in the thick, swirling snow they could not get a fix on their position. So they curled up in the cabin and waited out the storm; it lasted for five days and most of this time they slept.

A brief break in the weather enabled them at last to fix their position by sextant. They found that the island—they later learned it was named Dead Man's Island—lay between Kings Bay and their destination of Green Harbor, five miles to the north. With a little luck, they could make it to the coast.

The two cleared a runway and started the engine. The skis, however, sank into the soft, fresh snow, which fell without pause, and the craft would not move. Wilkins got out and pushed the Vega free, but when

The first men to cross the polar basin by plane, Carl Ben Eielson (left) and Sir Hubert Wilkins doff their hats to a crowd cheering their arrival in New York City on July 2, 1928. A week later the Lockheed Aircraft Company presented Wilkins with the painting at top right, which shows his Lockheed Vega about to land in Spitsbergen after its historic flight over the roof of the world from Point Barrow, Alaska.

he tried to haul himself into the cabin of the moving plane, he tumbled onto the ice. Eielson, in the cockpit, could not see into the rear of the cabin and he was airborne before he realized what had happened. He circled and landed. On the next lift-off, Wilkins again pushed the Vega, then tried to climb a rope ladder into the plane, but his numb hands failed him; for a few desperate moments, he held the ladder in his teeth as the craft accelerated, and was dragged across the snow like a dangling duffel bag. Again he let go. On the third try, however, Wilkins hooked a leg in the entry hatch of the cabin as he pushed the plane through the snow and then levered himself in with a long piece of driftwood from the beach as the craft took off. The men were airborne only a few moments before they saw the twin radio masts and the cottages of Green Harbor, where they set the plane down.

The long journey was greeted with a chorus of acclaim. Amundsen, who had thought it could not be done, acknowledged, "No flight has been made anywhere, at any time, which could be compared with it." Byrd called the flight the greatest ever in the Far North. Wilkins and Eielson stopped in Norway on their way to London and they were cheered, decorated and feted. Eielson's Norwegian heritage was proudly noted and a party Amundsen gave for them featured a cake adorned with a polar map showing their course. A few weeks later, Wilkins was knighted by King George V.

The first stage of the polar saga was complete. The Pole had been reached by air and traversed, the giant polar sea had been breached and the tale of polar land had been proved a myth. The way was now open for other pilots to put the explorers' findings to use, charting routes that in the years ahead would make transpolar flights between Europe and North America and between North America and Asia a reality. Eventually, the meteorological stations that Wilkins envisioned would be established in the Arctic, and the North Pole, as far as was possible, could be called conquered at last.

Last stop before the Pole

When the polar expedition led by Roald Amundsen and Lincoln Ellsworth arrived at Kings Bay, Spitsbergen, in April of 1925, none of the members doubted the magnitude of the task before them: a 1,700-mile flight over the unexplored territory at the top of the world. "A spirit almost of hilarity pervaded the camp," Ellsworth recalled, "testifying to the inner tension of all."

A shed belonging to the King's Bay Coal Company was cleared out to house the explorers. Amundsen christened it the Salon, and there for the next six weeks during off-duty hours the men feasted on such delicacies as cream buns and rum omelets, prepared by their cook, and listened to music. "A little gramophone provided us with all the jazz we desired," Amundsen noted wryly.

But there was also much hard work to be accomplished, as the hand-tinted photographs on these and the following pages show. The planes, which had come by ship, were assembled in the open air on the surface of the frozen harbor, and the equipment that had been carefully selected months earlier was brought ashore. Nothing had been left to chance, not even the kinds of boots to be worn: "If a man has had the opportunity of choosing his footwear," observed pilot Hjalmar Riiser-Larsen, "he will find it much easier to wear when exposed to hardship."

Each day the men checked the weather forecast and synchronized their watches to time signals beamed from the Eiffel Tower in Paris. On the afternoon of May 21, they taxied the planes across the ice. Then, with a roar of engines accompanied by shouts of encouragement, Amundsen and Ellsworth were off for the Pole. "If my pulse quickened then," Ellsworth wrote years later, "it was only with elation that at last I had accomplished my ambition in life."

Sailors from the Farm, one of the expedition's two vessels, clear a channel through the ice on arriving at Kings Bay. The passage enabled the Farm and her companion ship, the Hobby, to approach the shore.

Crewmen unloading crated equipment from the Hobby carefully lower one of the expedition's Dornier-Wal flying boats onto the ice.

Shortly after their arrival, expedition members haul a wing section across the ice from the ship to the mechanics' open-air workshop.

The footwear of the explorers includes several types of fur-lined ski shoes and rubber boots. The street shoes at far right were displayed in jest.

Meteorologists use a balloon and a theodolite to measure wind velocity.

Pilot Riiser-Larsen checks a Goerz sun compass for accuracy.

Roald Amundsen loads a folding canvas dinghy on a plane. Each of the expedition's two aircraft could carry 7,000 pounds of men and equipment.

Curious local coal company employees inspect one of the Dornier-Wals after it was assembled on the ice by the expedition's mechanics.

Their preparations completed, the explorers celebrate in their makeshift salon. Amundsen is seated at far right, with Ellsworth next to him.

On the day of departure, willing hands give Amundsen's heavily laden plane a final shove as it begins its takeoff run across the ice in Kings Bay.

2
Pioneering the great circle route

The 15,000 people who swarmed around the sun-baked airport at Rockford, Illinois, on the morning of July 26, 1928, were excited and proud, and they had reason to be. Rockford, hitherto a modest little city 90 miles northwest of Chicago, was about to launch itself into the vanguard of international aviation. The local folks had raised $25,000 to help finance a bold and visionary project conceived by Bert Hassell, a Rockford native who had taught military pilots to fly during World War I, test-flown new planes for Curtiss Aircraft and barnstormed about the Midwest for years. With another former World War I aviator, Parker "Shorty" Cramer, Hassell planned to fly a single-engined Stinson SM-1 Detroiter landplane—fitted with extra fuel tanks for the trip by his friend Eddie Stinson and named the *Greater Rockford*—to Stockholm via Canada, Greenland and Iceland. The flight was heralded in the newspapers as a demonstration of "practical air mindedness," showing the feasibility of an Arctic great circle air route between the American Midwest and Europe.

Such a route had been proposed as early as 1922 by Canadian explorer Vilhjalmur Stefansson, and it soon had many champions. (A great circle route is the shortest possible track between two points on the globe; it is so called because it is a section of an imaginary circle formed on the surface of the earth by a geometric plane passing through the earth's center.) Aviators, businessmen and military leaders alike saw the advantages in being able to fly to Europe or Asia over the top of the world. The distances would be shorter than for flights across the Atlantic or Pacific. And islands along the way could serve as bases for fuel depots, allowing journeys to be made in a series of short hops.

But pioneering an Arctic great circle route would not be all that easy. Hassell and Cramer faced enormous problems, the greatest of which was Greenland, an island 1,400 miles long and 700 miles wide that consists of a rim of high, barren mountains cupping an icecap thousands of feet thick. Greenland had never been traversed by air, and no one knew whether aircraft could attain the altitude necessary to cross the icecap or withstand its winds, which can reach 200 miles an hour.

Charles and Anne Lindbergh (rear cockpit) are welcomed by a naval officer in Washington, D.C., where the couple conferred with officials at the State Department before embarking on their 10,000-mile 1931 flight across the Arctic to the Orient.

Hassell and Cramer had done all they could to prepare for the journey. They had test-flown their Stinson all over the West and Midwest, and had sent a mechanic ahead to store fuel and lay out a runway in the snow near Sondre Strom Fjord on Greenland's west coast, where the University of Michigan had a geological and meteorological camp.

But the aviators had made some serious miscalculations. Moments after the Stinson roared out of sight of Rockford's cheering throng, the plane—overloaded with 400 gallons of fuel—brushed a knoll in a cornfield while struggling to climb in the hot, thin summer air. The *Greater Rockford's* undercarriage and one wing were smashed. Hassell, reporting cheerily that "nothing was hurt but our feelings," promised swift repair and a second attempt as soon as the plane was ready. Then Rockford supporters—40 per cent of them, including Hassell, of Scandinavian descent and naturally enthusiastic about a flight to the land of their ancestors—pitched in again, staging a theater benefit and a flying show as part of a "Rockford Won't Quit" fund-raising campaign. On August 16, the rebuilt craft, now carrying only 250 gallons of fuel, nosed into the Midwestern sky and set out on the first leg of its journey to Sweden. Seven hours later the Stinson landed safely in the town of Cochrane, in northeastern Ontario, for refueling.

After a two-day layover caused by bad weather, Hassell and Cramer headed northeast for the long haul, a 1,600-mile flight across the wilderness of northern Quebec Province and then over Davis Strait, which separates Canada's Baffin Island from Greenland. They were in the air for 20 hours, most of the time pinned between cloud layers that hid the ground and sea below and made it impossible for them to use their drift indicator. Then they broke out of the overcast and spotted the Greenland coast, its jagged mountains shielding the shimmering icecap.

They were looking for a large fjord—Sondre Strom Fjord—below Mount Evans, the site of the Michigan camp. But they did not know where they were, having deviated from their course when flying through the fog. They searched for hours and saw dozens of fjords, but none that looked like their 120-mile-long target, distinctive because of the island—named Simiutak, or "Stopper," by the Eskimos—that partly blocked its mouth. At length they established their position, but the search had taken four hours, fuel was running low and they were bucking head winds that rocked them out of their seats. Hassell decided to take the plane down. To his own surprise, he settled the Stinson onto the glacial ice without any damage, thus becoming the first pilot to land on Greenland's icecap. The exhausted men slumped in the cockpit, Hassell recalled later, "like two tired old barnstormers."

Barnstorming had never propelled them into such a fix. Seventy miles of crevassed ice, snow-covered mountains and steep-sided fjords separated them from the Michigan scientists. They radioed a report of their safe landing, but it was never received because of interference on the airwaves. Packing up what supplies they had—a rifle, a hatchet, some pemmican, a compass and a map of this unexplored area that, not

Hundreds of boosters wait for Bert Hassell and Parker Cramer to take off from Rockford, Illinois, on the aviators' second attempt to reach Sweden by the great circle route. Volunteers had lengthened the city's grass runway for the occasion, removing fence posts to give the 4,300-pound Stinson Detroiter a good safety margin.

surprisingly, lacked detail—they abandoned the *Greater Rockford* to the ice and set off on foot for Mount Evans.

While Hassell's wife and three small children, along with everyone else back home in Rockford, waited anxiously for news, the fliers spent two grim weeks on the Greenland icecap and the scrub-covered mountains that border it. They leaped crevasses and detoured around fjords and frozen canyons. Once, they stripped to wade a fast-moving glacial stream; their clothes remained dry, but the men had to walk for hours before they recovered from the bone-chilling cold. Another time, as they crossed a seemingly safe stretch of ground, Cramer sank to his waist in quicksand. Lacking sleeping bags, they rolled up in their overcoats at night. Whenever they could gather enough scrub and driftwood they made a fire to keep warm. And when their pemmican began to run low, they cut their ration to a meager five ounces a day.

At Mount Evans, the Michigan scientists had given Hassell and Cramer up for dead. But on September 2, Greenland Eskimos, passing near the scientists' camp on a caribou hunt, reported that they had seen smoke on the opposite shore of Sondre Strom Fjord. The scientists sent a boat across to investigate. To their delight, it returned with Hassell and Cramer, who were, as one observer reported, "gaunt after fourteen days of near starvation, but grinning happily."

The boosters back in Rockford celebrated with an impromptu parade. But Greenland was not yet finished with Hassell and Cramer. They were cruising down the fjord two days later on a motor sloop when the vessel struck a hidden rock and sank. Everyone aboard managed to reach safety on the shore, but the two pilots may not have felt altogether secure until they arrived in Denmark two weeks later, on their way home to an exultant reception. Still, they were not yet ready to quit. Hassell said the ordeal on the icecap had not shaken his belief that the Arctic route was the most logical way to fly to Europe. Cramer, too, was determined to make a successful flight across Greenland. And so, it turned out, were several other fliers, on both sides of the Atlantic.

Aviators from Europe—especially Northern Europe—were as enthusiastic as Americans about the possibilities of an Arctic great circle route. In the years immediately after Hassell and Cramer's attempt, British, Danish, Italian and German fliers all attacked the Greenland icecap or tried to navigate the entire east-west route across the Arctic between Europe and North America. The first successful great circle flight, which got under way in 1929, was made by a German, Wolfgang von Gronau.

Gronau, the son of a Prussian general, had distinguished himself as a pilot during World War I. After the War, he became the director of the most famous commercial flying school in Europe—the Deutsche Verkehrs Fliegerschule on the Baltic Sea—which was under the administration of the German Ministry of Transportation. Convinced of the commercial importance of an Arctic air route from Europe to North America, Gronau proposed to fly from Germany to the Faeroe Islands, north of Scotland, and then on to New York by way of Iceland, the southern tip of Greenland, the Davis Strait and Labrador. His proposal was received with little enthusiasm by the authorities at the Ministry of Transportation—until he made an unannounced and unauthorized flight from Sylt, a small island in the North Sea, to Iceland and back in July 1929. The feat persuaded the Ministry and Luft Hansa, the government-supported airline, to supply funds (albeit in secret, since their interest was in profitable future flights rather than adventurous flying displays) for an attempt at the Arctic air route.

Like his American contemporary Charles Lindbergh, Gronau was a modest and methodical pilot who left little to chance. The aircraft he chose for the flight was the very same sturdy Dornier flying boat—now fitted with 500-horsepower BMW engines—that had taken Amundsen almost to the Pole in 1926. In addition to standard navigational devices such as sun compasses, the Dornier carried the latest blind-flying equipment—an instrument called an artificial horizon that showed the craft's position in relation to the natural horizon, a precision altimeter and a

Hassell (right) and Cramer await rescue after the sloop conveying them down a Greenland fjord sank when it struck a rock. Only two days earlier the downed fliers had been picked up on the shore of the fjord, gaunt from 14 days of wandering the icecap.

gyrocompass, which gave a steady, reliable reading of the plane's heading. Fuel was stockpiled on the Faeroes, in Greenland and elsewhere along the proposed route. The three crewmen—a copilot, a radio operator and a mechanic—were all from Gronau's flying school.

The aviator shared Lindbergh's well-known penchant for keeping his own counsel. When the Dornier took off from Sylt on August 18, 1930, no one but Gronau—and of course the government, which was not ready to admit it publicly—knew how far he actually intended to fly. He had not even told his family or crew, explaining later that "I did not want blame attached to my name if the flight failed." His men got word that they were headed for North America only after they had completed a fog-hampered passage to Iceland on August 19. To the curious Icelanders, Gronau continued to insist that the flight was merely a training cruise and that he and his crew would soon return to the Continent.

Whatever doubt remained about the Germans' intentions disappeared when the big Dornier lifted off from Reykjavik harbor after a three-day weather delay and headed west toward Greenland. The clear sky that had tempted Gronau and his men aloft yielded to rain clouds and a strong north wind as they crossed the 200-mile-wide Denmark Strait. In order to see, Gronau sometimes climbed above the clouds and sometimes flew beneath them, only a few dozen yards over the storm-whipped water. But as they neared the coast, the clouds disappeared and a sudden rush of sunlight revealed a spectacular scene—great pinnacles of icebergs rising from the sea, with the wild white mountains behind, a vista Gronau found "barren and awful, though grand."

An apparent loss of power in the rear engine took their minds off the scenery until the mechanic located the problem—a malfunctioning tachometer—and corrected it. The nine-hour flight ended with a brief pass over Greenland's southern tip and a smooth landing in the ice-free harbor at Ivigtut on the west coast. Watching the plane's arrival, the resident Eskimos were, in Gronau's words, "stolidly amazed."

The weather on the next day's flight to Labrador was almost as bad as it had been on the Iceland-to-Greenland leg. Fog and clouds again dogged the Germans, and visibility was so poor that Gronau was forced once more to fly just above the waves. After six hours, the sight of huge, blue-green icebergs ahead told the fliers that land was near (icebergs are found in numbers only in the vicinity of the glaciers from which they are calved), and soon thereafter the Dornier crossed Labrador's high coastal cliffs. The Germans celebrated their arrival in North America with brandy all around, then landed for the night in the harbor at Cartwright.

Two days of fog-hampered hops down the Canadian coast brought Gronau and crew to Halifax, Nova Scotia. From there they headed straight for New York, triumphantly circled the Statue of Liberty and splashed down in the harbor just off the Battery, eight days and 47 flying hours after their departure from Germany.

Gronau had proved that a well-equipped flying boat, which required no landing fields, could fly between Europe and North America via the

Arctic, but the pilot himself doubted that this would lead to commercial routes across the frozen North anytime soon. While confessing to *The New York Times* that his flawless flight had fulfilled a lifelong dream, he added that dirigibles, with their greater range, were probably better suited for passenger travel. Planes—particularly landplanes—required "a tremendous amount of ground preparation and organization." For practical great circle flights, he said, airplanes would need more efficient engines so they could carry less fuel and larger payloads, as well as higher altitude capabilities to enable them to climb above storms. His own trailblazing feat, Gronau modestly averred, was merely "a training flight cruise with a flying boat that is somewhat out of date."

Though Gronau had flown an Arctic great circle route, he had avoided the Arctic's major obstacle: the Greenland icecap. In the summer of 1931, he set out to meet that challenge. Almost simultaneously Parker Cramer set out with the same goal in mind. Cramer, obsessed with the Arctic route, had tried a second great circle flight in 1929, using a twin-engined Sikorsky S-38 flying boat that sank at anchor in the stormy seas off Labrador. Now he had a Bellanca Pacemaker seaplane with a rela-

Police launches cluster around Wolfgang von Gronau's flying boat moments after it landed in New York Harbor. Just as Gronau was about to touch down, he spotted a floating timber directly ahead. He pulled his stick back and hurdled the obstacle, but the Dornier smacked down hard and stopped just 50 yards from Manhattan's Battery Park.

tively untried 225-horsepower Packard diesel radial engine. Sponsored by Trans America Airlines, which was interested in mail routes, he planned to fly from Detroit to Copenhagen via the Greenland icecap.

He and his radio operator, a Canadian named Oliver Pacquette, flew from Detroit to Greenland's west coast in short hops. Then on August 5, they winged across the icecap at 10,000 feet, reaching the island's east coast in just five hours. A few days after this triumph, they proceeded to Iceland and then to the Faeroe Islands without mishap. There, as they landed, they encountered Gronau taking off on the second leg of his own icecap attempt, and the pilots waved to each other.

Cramer and Pacquette's next stop was the Shetland Islands. On August 9, as they lifted the Bellanca off for the last leg to Copenhagen, they saw a man on the shore below waving a sheet of paper. Apparently thinking it only a note of congratulation, the two fliers headed off—straight into the savage North Sea gale that the man on the ground had been trying to warn them about: His paper was a radio message about the weather. Precisely what happened then—whether the plane's engine failed or whether Cramer was forced down by the storm—remains a mystery. Cramer and Pacquette were never seen again. Wreckage from the Bellanca was discovered a month later off the Shetland Islands.

Gronau, meanwhile, arrived in the small settlement of Angmagssalik on Greenland's east coast on August 13, and after being grounded by the weather for two days, set out across the icecap. Directed by the German government to "investigate the climatic and other conditions for a regular air route to America," he was piloting a new Dornier flying boat equipped with powerful 700-horsepower BMW VII engines. It was crewed by the men who had accompanied him the previous year.

The trip was a rough one. Heavily loaded with fuel, the Dornier took off from Scoresby Sound on August 15, laboring to gain the altitude required to clear the 10,000-foot mountains on the coast and the icecap itself. At times, Gronau flew within 600 feet of the ice, and he had to change course repeatedly to avoid the uncharted peaks that reared up before the plane. Midway across the cap, he was forced to fly blind through an hour-long snowstorm. He finally reached the west coast after a 10-hour struggle.

Gronau ended his epic flight in Chicago on September 1. When confronted with journalists' questions about the commercial viability of an Arctic great circle route, he still sounded unconvinced. "It is possible," he said, "but it would take a lot of money. There is always fog and always westerly winds." The icecap, the loneliest vista he had ever seen, could swallow any pilot unlucky enough to come down on its glistening expanse. There was nothing there, he added, but "ice and solitude."

While Cramer and Gronau were daring the Greenland icecap, the world's best-known aviator was pioneering the hazardous northerly course to Asia. Charles Lindbergh and his wife, Anne—whom he had taught to fly—had worked out an elaborate plan for a flight from the

United States to Tokyo, via northern Canada, Alaska and Siberia. The trip was sponsored by Pan American Airways, which was looking for overseas commercial routes, and it was marked by Lindbergh's characteristic blend of boldness, originality and painstaking preparation. The craft chosen was the most advanced long-distance seaplane then made, a Lockheed Sirius floatplane with a single 600-horsepower Wright Cyclone engine and extra fuel tanks that gave it a 2,100-mile range. It was fitted not only with blind-flying instruments and a two-way radio—Anne Lindbergh had acquired an operator's license—but also with a radio direction finder. This consisted of an antenna and a receiver with which the Lindberghs could pick up directional signals beamed from ground stations along their route and thus stay on course. Fuel was waiting at each scheduled stop, and in case of unscheduled landings, the Lindberghs carried everything they needed to be self-sufficient. They calculated that they could fly from New York to Tokyo in 12 hops, the longest leg 1,115 miles over Canada's unforgiving Barren Grounds.

After flying the Sirius from New York to Washington for clearances and passports, the Lindberghs headed for North Haven, Maine, to say good-by to their infant son, who had been left with Anne Lindbergh's parents. Then they began the trip proper, completing the first day's run on July 31, 1931, in Ottawa, where assorted experts tried to talk them into taking a safer route across the north country. The experts gave up only when Lindbergh threatened to fly to Europe and Asia via the Greenland icecap instead, a far more dangerous proposition. The next day, the pair started north on short flights across Ontario and Manitoba, stopping each night at ever more remote fur-trapping outposts.

On August 2 the Lindberghs reached the Northwest Territories, landing at Baker Lake, a community so isolated that the residents received their newspapers in batches of 365, one year late. The Lindberghs brought them up to date on the outside world and the next day took off for the village of Aklavik, more than 1,000 miles away.

On the flight to Aklavik, Anne Lindbergh got her first intimations of the unknown Arctic. The gray and treeless coast beneath them, she later wrote, "had no reality that could be recognized, measured and passed over. I knew that the white cloud bank out to sea hung over the ice pack—that it marked, like the fiery ring around an enchanted castle, the outer circle of a frozen kingdom we could not enter." It was 3 a.m. when they landed at Aklavik, waking most of the town and precipitating a chorus of howls from the packs of huskies tethered there.

The couple's first sustained encounter with the maddening mists of the summertime Arctic came on the 550-mile flight over the sea from Aklavik to Point Barrow, Alaska, Hubert Wilkins' old jumping-off point and the northern apex of their course. "Here a cloud and there a drizzle," Anne Lindbergh wrote, "here a wall and there, fast melting, a hole through which gleamed the hard metallic scales of the sea." Then came a climb into "white blankness" with no sight of land or sea or sky. Time and again Lindbergh descended beneath the fog, signaling to his

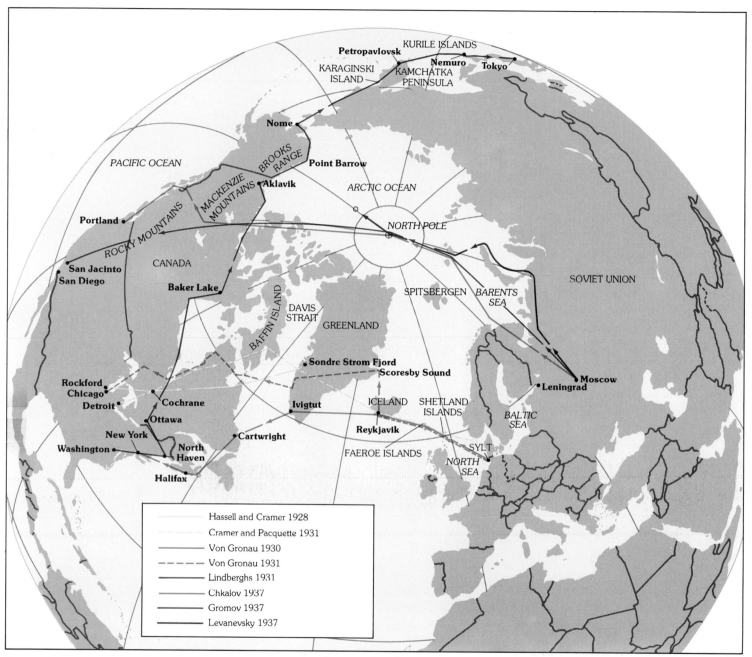

KURILE ISLANDS
Petropavlovsk
Nemuro
Tokyo
KARAGINSKI ISLAND
KAMCHATKA PENINSULA
Nome
PACIFIC OCEAN
BROOKS RANGE
Point Barrow
MACKENZIE MOUNTAINS
Aklavik
ARCTIC OCEAN
Portland
ROCKY MOUNTAINS
NORTH POLE
San Jacinto
San Diego
CANADA
SOVIET UNION
Baker Lake
SPITSBERGEN
BARENTS SEA
DAVIS STRAIT
BAFFIN ISLAND
GREENLAND
Rockford
Chicago
Detroit
Cochrane
Sondre Strom Fjord
Scoresby Sound
Moscow
Leningrad
Ottawa
Ivigtut
ICELAND
SHETLAND ISLANDS
BALTIC SEA
New York
Washington
North Haven
Cartwright
Reykjavik
FAEROE ISLANDS
SYLT
NORTH SEA
Halifax

	Hassell and Cramer 1928
	Cramer and Pacquette 1931
	Von Gronau 1930
	Von Gronau 1931
	Lindberghs 1931
	Chkalov 1937
	Gromov 1937
	Levanevsky 1937

During the late 1920s and the 1930s American, German and Russian aviators sought new air routes between Europe, North America and Asia via the Arctic. Each of the pilots listed below set out to fly a great circle route, the shortest path between any two points on the globe. But wind, weather and other obstacles caused them to deviate slightly from their planned courses, and in the case of two, Cramer and Hassell, to miss their goal entirely.

wife to reel in the trailing antenna of their radio. They were flying so near the waves that they risked snapping off the weight at its end. The fog lifted on their approach to Barrow. They landed in a lagoon, got out of the Sirius and were greeted by a crowd of Eskimos "not with a shout," Anne Lindbergh wrote, "but a slow, deep cry of welcome."

At Barrow the Lindberghs learned that the ship en route to the settlement with the year's eagerly awaited supplies, as well as fuel for their plane, was ice-locked 100 miles away, waiting for the wind change that would open the pack and release it. The couple settled in for what would turn out to be a three-day stay, dining their first night on roast reindeer and canned vegetables and offering to help their host with the dishes.

On August 10—one day after Parker Cramer vanished in the North

A flying family's Arctic misadventures

Aviator George R. Hutchinson wanted to prove that flying was safe for everyone. In August 1932, he boarded a twin-engined Sikorsky amphibian with his wife, his two daughters, aged six and eight, and a four-man crew, including a cameraman—and took off from New York for London via the Arctic.

The family flew across New Brunswick and Labrador and on to Greenland's west coast. Here they encountered an obstacle in the form of Danish officials who said that the Hutchinsons' "daredevil experiment" could not continue because of its hazards, especially for the wife and daughters. But after Hutchinson paid a $178 fine, the flight was permitted to proceed, not across Greenland's icecap as planned, but along the relatively safer southern coast.

Carrying only minimal survival gear and ignoring a forecast of snow, the Hutchinsons embarked on their swing around the coast. They flew into the storm en route to the village of Angmagssalik. With visibility nearing zero, and the wings icing up, Hutchinson descended until he was skimming the offshore ice. He lacked sufficient fuel to turn back, and in desperation came down on the

water, barely missing several ice floes. He then began taxiing along the coast toward the town 50 miles away.

After a half hour, the plane began to ship water and Hutchinson steered toward the shore. The Sikorsky just made it, nosing up to a rock. The Hutchinsons and crew grabbed what possessions and equipment they could and scrambled ashore as the plane continued to take on water. They climbed to a promontory, built a shelter out of rocks and spent the night huddled together. In the morning they found that the partially submerged plane had been crushed by drifting ice.

Unable to transmit on their radio, the Hutchinsons burned strips of movie film in the hope the flames would be spotted by a passing ship. During their second night on the island, the skipper of a trawler searching for them saw what looked like a red flare on the shore. He signaled a message with his lamp: "If you are the Hutchinson Flying Family, show two more lights." Two immediately blazed. The captain waited until dawn and then sent a boat to pick them up.

All were suffering from the cold but were otherwise all right—and far luckier than they knew. Discussing the rescue a few days later, the captain complimented Hutchinson on his speedy response to the message. "What message?" the pilot replied. It turned out none of the stranded party had understood the signal, but they had chosen that precise moment to burn two strips of film.

Home again, Hutchinson said that he could not understand why newspapers had criticized him: "I did not subject my family to any more hazards than if they were traveling in an automobile. We are depending on the younger generation to carry aviation on in the future, so why object to my taking the children?"

George R. Hutchinson (second from left) and his family, clad in suede britches, prepare to take off from New York with their crew on a 4,000-mile flight to London. The family had already won fame visiting by air the capitals of the 48 states.

Sea—the Lindberghs decided not to wait any longer for the supply ship. They had, Lindbergh thought, enough fuel to fly the 520 miles to Nome. But now they came up against something they had failed to consider in planning their trip: The long days of the Arctic summer were beginning to shorten. At 8:30 p.m. they were still two hours short of Nome when dusk caught up with them, accompanied by fog. The approach of night over the northern wilderness filled Anne Lindbergh with "the terror of a savage seeing the first eclipse." A message from the Nome radio operator promised flares to light their landing, but Lindbergh chose to come down for the night in an inlet rather than risk flying in darkness and fog over the Brooks Range. After a tricky downwind landing, the Lindberghs improvised a bed in the plane's baggage compartment. They had just fallen asleep when they were roused with a start by the sound of someone calling them. They looked out and saw beside the pontoons two small boats roofed with skins. From inside the boats stared Eskimo faces. "Hello," one of the visitors said. "We hunt duck."

Lindbergh replied brightly, "Get many ducks?" With this, the conversation stalled, and the aviators went back to bed.

They reached Nome safely in the morning and took on a full load of fuel for the 1,000-mile overwater flight to their next refueling point, the Siberian island of Karaginski. When they arrived there on August 15, they were greeted by fur trappers and a small, orphaned brown bear that served as the local pet. Their hosts fed them wild strawberries and milk and informed them that it was now Saturday, August 16, instead of Friday, August 15: Having crossed the 180th meridian—the international date line   the Lindberghs had lost a full day. The next day they flew south to Petropavlovsk, a fishing village on the coast with a beautiful deep harbor and, on the hills that rose from it, houses brightly painted in traditional Russian style. They lingered for three days, preparing for the thorniest part of their course, a long southerly passage over the notoriously foggy Kuriles, the chain of islands linking Siberia's Kamchatka Peninsula to Hokkaido, Japan's second largest island.

The Kuriles lived up to their billing, and the journey was frightening, although the Sirius was guided by Japanese radio operators most of the time. About halfway along the 1,000-mile stretch the Sirius hit a wall of fog that concealed the mountains, making an immediate descent essential. Anne Lindbergh watched her husband push back the cockpit cover and don his goggles, "the familiar buckling on of armor" that signaled another joust with the elements. Alternating between visual and instrument flight, Lindbergh groped his way down through the mist, skirting the mountains in search of a patch of sea to land on. Finally, after several tries that left his wife white-knuckled and momentarily determined to fly no more, he found a hole in the fog and dived for it, leveling off just above the water and landing with a series of bounces that buckled the spreader bars between the pontoons. They were at Ketoi Island, 100 miles northeast of Brouton Island, where their fuel was stored.

The Lindberghs spent a rough night in the wave-rocked Sirius, wak-

北門木室

Japanese boatmen help Charles Lindbergh (standing on pontoon) anchor the Sirius at Nemuro, a small fishing port on eastern Hokkaido. The 10,000 townspeople who turned out hailed the American couple with sirens and a thunderous cheer of "Banzai!"

ing in the morning to find the ship *Shinshuru Maru,* sent by the Japanese government, standing by to assist them. Sailors helped Lindbergh repair the plane and then towed it to the calm waters of Brouton Bay.

One day later, the Lindberghs took off for Nemuro, on the eastern tip of Hokkaido. Relentless fog and rain forced the plane down twice en route. One landing was at a tiny willow- and pine-covered island called Kunashiri, where three of the inhabitants—a fisherman, his father and his son—fed them and courteously sent them on their way. On August 23 the Lindberghs finally arrived in Nemuro, where a crowd of 10,000 welcomed them. The unshaven pilot and his first mate were "dirty, as you see," he said to the assembled newspapermen, "but not tired." He let it be known that he appreciated the fine weather "because we had only a half-hour's gasoline left." After refueling, the Lindberghs flew on to Tokyo, there to be greeted by another throng.

The Americans had flown the Arctic great circle route from New York to Tokyo, the first time anyone had attempted such a feat, in 83 hours' air time. Lindbergh told reporters in Tokyo that the flight had been a "pleasure trip" and added with his customary exactness that their altitude had ranged from a high of 7,000 feet to a low of 57. Despite his modest assessment, the Lindberghs' flight was a spectacular one. The brilliance and precision they displayed, however, would soon be matched by fliers from the nation with the longest Arctic coastline in the world.

The Soviet Union had remained curiously silent during the years when aerial explorers such as Byrd and Wilkins and Gronau and Lindbergh were pioneering in the northern latitudes, but in the mid-1930s it became apparent that Soviet silence did not connote inaction. On the contrary. During the early part of the decade, the Russians quietly geared up for an aeronautical exploit that no one had yet dared—a nonstop airplane flight over the North Pole from Europe to North America. By 1937, they had the aircraft to do it—the single-engined ANT.25. Designed by famed aeronautical engineer Andrei N. Tupolev, it was a remarkable machine, with a glider-like wingspan of 112 feet, a fuel capacity of 2,000 gallons and a range of more than 6,000 miles.

The crew, chosen by Stalin himself, consisted of pilot Valery Chkalov, copilot Georgi Baidukov and navigator-radioman Alexander Beliakov, aviators who had been training for just such an opportunity. They had only recently flown across the Soviet Arctic by what they called the Stalin Route, and the flight west was to crown their efforts. On June 18, 1937, they took off in the ANT.25 from Moscow with the announced goal of flying to Oakland, California, via the Pole.

Chkalov and Baidukov alternated at the controls as they flew northeast of Leningrad and out over the Barents Sea, gradually ascending to 6,500 feet, the best they could do with their heavy load; in addition to fuel, the ANT.25 carried a tent, an electric stove, skis, rifles, sleeping bags, rations for six weeks and oxygen—the last to be used at altitudes where thin air could cause confusion and illness. After 10 uneventful hours, they ran into a cloud bank. Ice—"aviation's fiercest enemy," said Baidukov—soon began to form in the carburetor and on the wings and windows. The engine began to shudder. The airmen activated their deicing pump, which affected only the engine and propeller. But to melt the dangerously heavy ice from the wings and tail, they had to take the ANT.25—now lightened by the consumption of some of its fuel—up above the clouds to 8,200 feet, where the brilliant Arctic sun could do the job. A few hours later the clouds rose to more than 13,000 feet, and it was becoming difficult to stay on top of them.

Baidukov tried to hold a northerly course while struggling to climb. "No one can understand what pilots go through in the face of natural forces," he wrote in his chronicle of the flight. "You want to weep from vexation. The thought of your plane turning into an iceberg—the thought of surrendering helplessly to nature—is horrible." He managed to get to 13,600 feet and once more leveled off above the clouds.

The men, already fatigued from 11½ hours of flying, began to feel the chill, stiffness and clumsiness that are symptoms of oxygen deprivation. But they dared not draw now upon their oxygen supply, knowing that they would need it more later. The ANT.25 reached 14,000 feet and they flew steadily on through the unending daylight. It finally became necessary to take short, occasional whiffs of the oxygen. Thus refreshed, they returned to the pipes that all three smoked.

Twenty-seven hours after their takeoff they passed over the North Pole, "a gigantic wilderness of ice crisscrossed in all directions by fissures," wrote Baidukov, who was flying at the time. "The Pole does not mean a damned thing to the airman. We have passed over it and that is that." Chkalov, the leader of the expedition, was asleep; the lack of oxygen had caused an old leg injury to ache miserably, increasing his fatigue, and he had not even asked to be awakened for the historic moment. The pilots did, however, radio North Pole greetings to Stalin.

Clouds massed in their path again as they flew on toward northwestern Canada, forcing the aviators to climb to 18,700 feet—as high as the plane could go with its fuel load. But they were unable to rise above the sea of fleece. Baidukov tried unsuccessfully to find a way around the clouds; defeated, he flew on instruments. Suddenly there was a new crisis. Steam from the radiator struck the windscreen and froze. Baidukov reached outside into 100-mile-per-hour winds and chopped the ice away with a knife. Then he saw that the water-level gauge for the radiator read zero; the pipe feeding water to the radiator was frozen and the engine was in danger of burning out. Chkalov and Beliakov hastily pumped the reserve radiator tank but got nothing; its contents were

A crowd of onlookers braves a drizzle to get a glimpse of a Soviet ANT.25 after it flew from Moscow to the state of Washington in 62½ hours in 1937. The crowd materialized "as if by magic" and "cheered the fliers lustily," one newspaper reported.

frozen as well. Chkalov seized their container of drinking water and cracked the thick layer of ice that had formed inside. Without hesitating, he poured the lifesaving fluid into the reserve tank and began pumping. Slowly the water-level needle inched up as he revved the engine and its heat began to warm the pipe and restore the flow. They were safe.

The weather cleared as they sighted land—islands off northwestern Canada. They had been in the air for more than two days.

The route south into Canada took them over the cloud-covered Mackenzie Mountains, the beginning of the mountain chains that traverse the western part of the continent. To avoid the peaks, the Russians had to stay above 13,000 feet—yet the oxygen they would need to remain conscious at that altitude was running out. Baidukov decided he had to get away from the mountains. He turned west and headed across the Rockies toward the Pacific, where he knew he could descend safely to a more comfortable altitude. He climbed another 5,000 feet and, as earlier, could not shake the clouds. Chkalov spelled him at the controls, flying blind, struggling to keep alert. Then the oxygen ran out and Baidukov began a cautious descent, trying, as historian John Grierson put it, "to strike the happy medium between falling unconscious and flying the plane into a mountain." An hour later, a break in the clouds showed the sea beneath. The Russians had cleared the Rockies.

Flying on instruments through the night, they reached an Army field

Five weeks after their flight to Vancouver, Washington, pilot Valery Chkalov (right) and his two crewmen receive a hero's welcome from their families and dignitaries in Moscow. The three were then escorted to the Kremlin and given the Order of Lenin.

in Vancouver, Washington, on the morning of June 20. After the plane had rolled to a stop, Chkalov staggered out of the cockpit and reached for a cigarette. They had flown 5,507 nonstop miles in 62½ hours, an astonishing accomplishment by any measure and a stunning confirmation of Soviet prowess in the air. The three crewmen shrugged affably in response to the questions they were besieged with—none of them spoke English—and then repaired to the home of the base commander, Brigadier General George C. Marshall, the same man who would later serve as U.S. Army Chief of Staff and Secretary of State. When an interpreter was found and the three Russians could communicate, they had only two requests—water and some cognac.

Russia launched another three-man crew on a nearly identical flight less than a month later. Flying an ANT.25 much like the one Chkalov and Baidukov had piloted, airman Mikhail Gromov made even better time, passing over the Pole in a snowstorm only 23 hours after leaving Moscow. Gromov followed a similar course to Canada but pushed on all the way to San Diego before fog forced him to turn around and land in a cow pasture near San Jacinto, 90 miles east of Los Angeles. Gromov had flown 6,262 miles in 62 hours and 20 minutes, a new nonstop distance record.

The Russian pilot and his two companions made a hit in California. They greeted the startled ranchers who reached them first by handing out printed cards conveying their most urgent requirements—"bath," "eat" and "sleep." After these needs were satisfied, the three were invited to Hollywood, where they toured a movie studio and did what The New York Times said "most visitors want to do"—they met Shirley Temple. Aviation experts assumed that the Russian flights were designed to study the feasibility of transpolar air travel, but Pravda suggested a more ominous motive: "Let our foreign enemies who threaten us with war know," the Soviet newspaper declared in an apparent reference to Nazi talk about expanding Germany's borders, "that we are much nearer their capitals than we are to Portland or San Jacinto."

In August it was Sigismund Levanevsky's turn. Unlike the other Soviet fliers, the blond, 35-year-old Levanevsky had visited the United States and spoke English. Because of his flying feats, Levanevsky was called "the Lindbergh of Russia," and Americans remembered him fondly as the man who had rescued their around-the-world flier James Mattern when Mattern's plane went down in Siberia in 1933. Levanevsky's assignment was to take the Chkalov and Gromov flights one step further: He and five crewmen would fly a large military plane across the Pole to Fairbanks, Alaska, and on to New York. The red and blue ANT.4, a cousin of the ANT.25, measured 125 feet from wing tip to wing tip; it was powered by four 680-horsepower M-17 engines and had been designed as a bomber. It could carry up to 25 people.

Abandoning their customary secrecy, Russian officials permitted Western journalists to witness the plane's smooth lift-off on August 12. Looking "unconcernedly confident," according to The New York

The second trio of Soviet aviators within a month to fly an ANT.25 from Moscow to Southern California ride down Moscow's Gorki Street soon after the men returned home. To welcome the heroes, thousands of Muscovites lined the sidewalks and crowded into buildings hung with giant portraits of pilot Mikhail Gromov (opposite, above) and his comrades.

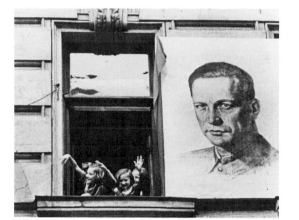

Times, Levanevsky announced just before he climbed aboard that he expected to reach Alaska, where the weather was reported good, in 30 hours. He reached the North Pole in 19½ hours, but a message transmitted 300 miles farther on indicated that something was seriously awry: "Motor 34," it began, indicating in code that one engine was malfunctioning. "Flying heavily against 100-kilometer wind. Losing altitude from 6,000 meters to 4,300 meters." Moments later there came a more urgent transmission that broke off in midsentence. All that could be heard were the code numbers "48-3400." This meant, "We are going to land in . . ." Then the radio fell silent.

No one knew what had happened. Had Levanevsky been forced down by ice on the wings? The failure of one engine would not be enough to bring the ANT.4 down; had a second motor given out? If the men were alive somewhere on the ice, they could presumably survive on their emergency rations until they were found. But what if the heavy plane had crashed through the ice or plunged straight into the sea?

In the absence of any further radio messages it seemed likely that the

six Russians were either stranded on a floe or dead. The crowd waiting to greet them at the Fairbanks airport gave up after several hours and quietly dispersed. The search, complicated by the Arctic's foggy August weather, began immediately. Joe Crosson, a well-known Alaskan bush pilot, was among the first to volunteer. James Mattern, the aviator Levanevsky had rescued in Siberia, flew up from Los Angeles in hopes of returning the favor. In Russia, where long lines of people anxiously waited for the daily papers, it was announced that planes and ships would soon be sent to join the search. But the area to be searched was so vast and perilous that few planes—and few pilots—were up to it. Four days after Levanevsky's disappearance came the welcome news that the man who was probably better qualified for the job than anyone else alive would spearhead the search: Sir Hubert Wilkins was preparing to fly north from Point Barrow in a Consolidated Catalina flying boat purchased by the Russian government.

Wilkins, Canadian pilot Herbert Hollick-Kenyon and a small crew arrived at Coppermine on the Canadian Arctic coast on August 21. The next day they began systematically crisscrossing an area 1,200 miles long and 400 miles wide on the Alaskan side of the Pole. Weather stations manned by Russians, Canadians and Americans furnished meteorological data that enabled the aviators to take advantage of the infrequent breaks in the fog, and they remained aloft as long as 21 hours at a time. They found no sign of the Russians or their plane. By late

Workers fuel pilot Sigismund Levanevsky's massive ANT.4 bomber for an attempt to fly from Moscow to New York City via Fairbanks, Alaska, in August 1937. The craft carried 18 tons (6,000 gallons) of fuel in its wing tanks.

Soviet Air Force Commander Jacob Alksnis (right) bids a fraternal farewell to Levanevsky on August 12 just before the young pilot took off for New York. Nineteen hours later, Levanevsky and his five crewmen vanished over the Arctic, setting off a fruitless seven-month search.

September, with the seasonal freeze beginning, the winter darkness coming on and seaplane landings no longer feasible, Wilkins broke off and went to Washington to discuss matters with the Soviet ambassador.

A few weeks later, he was back in the Arctic with a Lockheed L10 Electra skiplane. Convinced that the men might still be alive, he flew a succession of search missions illuminated only by the bright moonlight reflected off the snow and ice. Through January and February and March he doggedly continued the hunt, which by this time had become the most expensive and exhaustive Arctic air search ever mounted. Russian search teams, operating primarily from Siberia, had suffered six crashes. Moscow finally ordered a halt to the search in mid March. Not a single trace of the missing men was ever found.

Wilkins later calculated that his efforts had taken him over 170,000 square miles of the Arctic Ocean, most of which had never been seen before. It had been possible because of the rapid evolution in Arctic aviation that had occurred in the nine years since he and Ben Eielson flew from Point Barrow to Spitsbergen. "I realized," he wrote, "how many of my hopes and dreams of my early years had somehow touched me in the search for Levanevsky. I had flown thousands of miles—not in a rickety crate but in sturdy, powerful planes. We had not had one crash, but had flown for months in perfect safety. Never had we been out of touch with the rest of the world, because our short-wave radio had kept us in contact with every development in the search at all times. We had not flown by guesswork into unknown weather conditions, because the meteorological resources of several governments were at our disposal hourly, and their science enabled us to save many precious hours and avoid needless risks."

Levanevsky's death furnished proof that the Arctic had not yet been tamed for airplanes, but the equipment and support systems for safe flight were available. And in fact, flights over the Pole would become commonplace within a decade, for military aircraft during World War II, and later for commercial aviation. ～

3

"To the end of south"

For the elite cadre of aerial explorers who had made the first flights of discovery in the Arctic—for Richard Byrd and Hubert Wilkins, Roald Amundsen and Lincoln Ellsworth, and Ben Eielson—the distance from one end of the earth to the other could be traversed in a single leap of the imagination. These aeronautical frontiersmen took their satisfaction not in blazing trails for commercial routes but in the heady thrill of discovery itself, in beholding and, for a moment perhaps, possessing a place where man had never walked. They had served their apprenticeship in the Arctic, and its lure had faded. To these men the route-charting flights by such pilots as Charles Lindbergh and Wolfgang von Gronau were like road building in the wilderness. The aerial explorers looked now to the south for adventure, to a land with space and mystery enough for all of them: Antarctica.

In many ways the South Polar regions are the opposite of the Arctic. Antarctica is, as Ellsworth put it, "a continent surrounded by oceans rather than an ocean girt by continents." That continent—one and a half times the size of the United States—is five million square miles of icecap pierced by towering chains of mountains (*map, page 80*). It is colder than the ocean-warmed Arctic, and its weather is fiercer, marked by freakish blizzards and the strongest winds on earth.

Antarctica is so forbidding, in fact, that in 1920 virtually nothing was known about it. For 100 years, whalers in search of the migrating leviathans dared the ice pack when it opened in spring, and venturesome sailors had charted the continent's fringes. Only the most intrepid of old-school explorers had penetrated the interior: Roald Amundsen had led a sled party to the Pole in 1911, beating by only a few weeks the British explorer Robert Scott, who died of cold and starvation on his return trip. Now it was the turn of the new breed of airborne explorers to hazard the interior, and the first to try were Richard Byrd and Hubert Wilkins, gentlemanly rivals with different styles and different goals.

The million-dollar, impeccably organized Byrd company got under way ahead of Wilkins' much more modest party. A square-rigged sailing ship, the *City of New York,* bearing 32 of the Byrd expedition's 83 men, left Hoboken, New Jersey, in late August 1928 and headed for New

Lincoln Ellsworth's ship, the Wyatt Earp, plows through ice-clogged waters off Antarctica in 1934. Lashed to the deck is the Northrop Gamma in which Ellsworth hoped to cross the continent.

Zealand. There she would join three other expedition ships and together they would sail for Antarctica. Byrd had thought of everything. *New York Times* writer Russell Owen, the only journalist on the trip, noted in his departure-day dispatch that the ship also carried alcohol, forbidden to Americans at the time by Prohibition, but necessary, Byrd declared, for medicinal reasons.

Owen, who was to win a Pulitzer Prize for his coverage of Byrd's 14 months on the foreign continent, knew as Byrd did that the Antarctic was a far more formidable test than the Arctic. The silent white expanse, he wrote, was a "grim, perilous country which tries the hearts of all who venture within her gates of ice." Expedition members, he continued, could expect "the most trying experiences which men can willingly encounter in days of peace."

The achievement of Byrd's principal objectives—the geographical exploration of the continent and a flight to the South Pole—required much more than the felicitous blend of skill, equipment and luck that had marked his round-trip sortie between Spitsbergen and the North Pole. What was needed was a carefully designed operation, one that could succeed in an implacably hostile environment. Byrd, a brilliant organizer and leader, recognized this from the outset. With the financial backing of John D. Rockefeller Jr., Edsel Ford, the National Geographic Society, the American Geographical Society and *The New York Times,* among others, he put together an expedition that had all the latest gear and scientific equipment, some of it specially designed for use in the Antarctic. Before the expedition could succeed, however, a base camp had to be established. By the end of December Byrd's eager troops were digging into the snow and constructing the underground world of Little America on the Ross Ice Shelf, which projected 500 miles into the Ross Sea. But meanwhile, Hubert Wilkins had beaten Byrd into the air.

Wilkins' expedition had arrived in Antarctica by whaling ship in early November and set up its own camp at Deception Island, a steep-sided volcanic outcropping near the tip of Graham Land, the northwestern extremity of Antarctica. The expedition, backed by the American Geographical Society, the Detroit Aviation Society and the Hearst news service, among others, consisted only of Wilkins, Alaska pilots Ben Eielson and Joe Crosson, an engineer and a radio operator. Wilkins' Lockheed Vega had been overhauled, and the Lockheed Company, which appreciated the publicity from Wilkins' Arctic flight, had supplied a second Vega at cost; both airplanes could be fitted with wheels, skis or floats. In these craft Wilkins hoped to make a series of reconnaissance missions that would result in the discovery of a suitable site for an advance base 600 miles to the south. Then, with the base established, he would attempt a 2,000-mile flight across unexplored territory to the Bay of Whales, close to Byrd's Little America. His objective was to gain knowledge not only of the terrain, but of the weather, as part of his long-cherished dream of establishing meteorological stations at both ends of the globe. He had no intention of trying for the Pole and could offer Byrd—who was alarmed that Wilkins might precede him there—assurances that he had no plans to upstage him.

The weather had been unusually warm, melting the snow on the island's lower slopes and breaking up the ice in the bay where the whaling ship was going about its business. Because the thaw made the Vegas' skis useless, Wilkins installed wheels on the planes and took off for a survey flight from a hillside composed of volcanic tuff. With Eielson at the controls and the explorer in the observer's seat, the Vega managed to clear the slope and achieve aviation's debut in the Antarctic. They hoped to spot a more likely landing area from the air, but they were driven back down by clouds after only a few minutes.

Ten days later, the weather relented enough to permit more extended survey flights, again in search of a better airstrip, but the terrain proved to be either mountainous or pitted with crevasses. Returning from one of these, Eielson decided to land on the bay ice, which he judged firm enough now to support the plane. He touched down smoothly but then taxied onto soft ice and plunged partially through a hole into the water. The pilot scrambled out, but it took several hours of effort by 20 crewmen from the whaling ship to haul the Vega back onto firm ice and drag it to a spot where the engine could be dried and cleaned of salt. Crosson encountered another hazard after he fitted floats on one of the planes and tried a water landing near the ship.

A hybrid craft for ground and sky

Douglas Mawson, leader of a 1911-1914 Australian expedition to the Antarctic, was a forward-thinking man. At a time when the airplane was still something of a novelty, he ordered one from the Vickers company in England to take with him to Antarctica. His plan was to use it not only for survey work, but on the ground as a sled-pulling tractor.

Before the expedition left Australia, however, the plane crashed on a trial flight. Though repairs were made, Mawson decided against flying it in Antarctica; instead, shorn of its wings, it would be used as a tractor. But Mawson had not counted on the continent's weather, for which the propeller-driven craft was no match. In the end he was forced to abandon it when its pistons seized and broke.

The "air-tractor sledge," fitted with runners and wheels, awaits shipment to Antarctica.

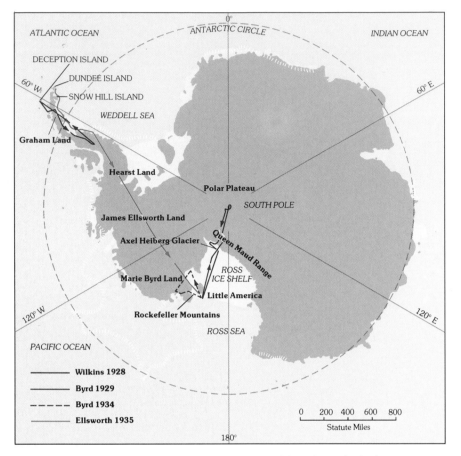

ATLANTIC OCEAN
ANTARCTIC CIRCLE
INDIAN OCEAN
0°
DECEPTION ISLAND
DUNDEE ISLAND
60° W.
SNOW HILL ISLAND
60° E
WEDDELL SEA
Graham Land
Hearst Land
Polar Plateau
SOUTH POLE
James Ellsworth Land
Axel Heiberg Glacier
Queen Maud Range
ROSS
ICE SHELF
Marie Byrd Land
Little America
120° W
120° E
Rockefeller Mountains
ROSS SEA
PACIFIC OCEAN

Wilkins 1928
Byrd 1929
Byrd 1934
Ellsworth 1935

0   200   400   600   800
Statute Miles

180°

This map traces the routes of major Antarctic flights between 1928 and 1935. Hubert Wilkins flew the 600-mile length of Graham Land in 1928. A year later Richard Byrd reached the South Pole from Little America. In 1934 Byrd covered 777 miles of previously unseen territory. The next year Lincoln Ellsworth made the first trans-Antarctic flight—2,200 miles from Dundee Island to Little America.

Thousands of sea birds had been attracted by the whaler's activities, and the plane struck and killed several of them; fortunately no damage was done to engine or craft.

Wilkins realized his best bet was to improve the slope from which they had been taking off. Laboriously, the men scraped at the tuff until they had a cindery, curving strip 40 feet wide, 2,500 feet long, with two 20-degree bends. This was hardly ideal, but it did allow Wilkins and Eielson to make the first extended exploratory flight in Antarctica. On a bright, sparkling December 20, they zigzagged down the runway and took off.

Flying southwest at 125 miles per hour over the strait separating Deception Island and Graham Land, they climbed to 6,000 feet and began scanning the horizon for the plateau that was listed on their charts as 4,000 to 6,000 feet high. What they encountered was an icy plain at least 2,000 feet higher than the charts showed. Eielson gradually gained altitude until the Vega crested it at 8,200 feet.

Heading south over the plateau, they crossed country whose surprisingly varied colors had been hidden from men's eyes until this moment. Jagged rocks rose in dark clusters from a sea of white. Everything, Wilkins wrote, was "frozen and still, black and blue-black and black-green and glittering white." Winging over Graham Land and passing over the offshore shelf ice in the Weddell Sea, they looked down on "huge crevasses into which our machine could have fallen and left no trace," wrote Wilkins.

Antarctica from here on was a geographic blank, which meant that an explorer could exercise his privilege of naming the features he saw. Wilkins, as Byrd was to do later, seized this opportunity to flatter his backers. He called the high plain the Detroit Aviation Society Plateau; a range of coastal peaks was named the Lockheed Mountains and the body of water hard by became Mobiloil Bay; a broad expanse stretching out of sight to the south was called Hearst Land.

After five hours and 600 miles of flying, and with half their fuel gone, Wilkins and Eielson turned around for the trip back to Deception Island. The weather had been kind so far, but they could see several areas of clouds and the signs of a storm developing along their homeward course. As Wilkins and Eielson flew northward, they reflected with pleasure on the flight. They were convinced that Graham Land was not in fact the peninsula that everyone imagined, but a series of islands separated by iced-over straits and channels. (This conclusion stirred a brisk debate among geographers before it was finally refuted in 1940.) And Wilkins calculated that they had discovered eight previously unknown islands and—more useful for his own purposes—several places where a skiplane might safely land.

The incipient storm they had spied earlier appeared to be building, and as they passed the Graham Land shore, they could see that clouds extended over Deception Island. Eielson flew at 5,000 feet to stay above the weather. If he could not get down to the improvised runway, the two fliers faced a range of unpleasant possibilities, the best of which was a long and chilly walk.

But as Eielson circled the cloud cover above the base, a hole opened and he dived into it. Flying in tight spirals to avoid the mountains, he battled to hold the Vega steady in the turbulent air. A few moments later, just 10 hours after takeoff, he was safely on the ground.

A radio call to Wilkins the next day showed that at least one keenly interested party was aware of his accomplishment. "Hearty congratulations on your splendid flight," read the message from Richard Byrd, who had heard about it on the radio. "Don't forget you will find a warm welcome if you fly to our base." But Wilkins would have to defer any such flight for at least another year. Unable to establish the advance skiplane base necessary for a trans-Antarctic flight and with the weather worsening daily, he called it quits for the season, vowing to return 10 months later, when ice conditions would be better. He left the two Vegas behind, tied down securely to withstand the wind, and sailed back to South America in February. Across the continent in Little America, Byrd and his men were settling in for the winter.

Lying eight miles in from the edge of the Ross Ice Shelf, the base contained everything needed to sustain life in this hostile land. Included in the three clusters of buildings were an administration center, a mess hall, living quarters, laboratories, kennels for the 94 sled dogs, blacksmith and sled-repair shops, and, of course, an aviation repair shop, located near the runway marked out on the ice. There was even a 3,000-book library.

Byrd intended to spend the few weeks still left in the 1929 flying season in preparation, reconnaissance and flight testing. The plan called for the winter months—April to November in Antarctica—to be devoted to collecting and analyzing meteorological and geological data, with the climactic flight to the Pole to follow as early as practicable during the summer season.

The expedition would have three planes at its disposal—a single-engined Fairchild with folding wings, a single-engined Fokker Universal and a larger Ford Tri-motor. The last was named the *Floyd Bennett* after Byrd's pilot on the North Pole flight, who had died the year before of pneumonia. By mid-January, work had proceeded far enough for the pilots to begin initial flight tests with the Fairchild, the first of the crated planes to be assembled. The serious business of exploration got under way on January 27 with a five-hour flight in the Fairchild by Byrd, pilot Bernt Balchen, who had served with Roald Amundsen in the Arctic, and radio operator Harold June. Balchen ascended swiftly after a 30-second run and headed east toward the mysterious land beyond the ice shelf.

With visibility good, the excited explorers passed a chain of low

An unloading crew rests on its dog sleds near two supply ships for Little America, the Eleanor Bolling (far left) and the City of New York. The ships were moored together alongside the Ross Ice Shelf on January 29, 1929, despite the danger of a breakup of the already softening ice.

mountains Robert Scott had named the Alexandras. Soon they were flying through haze, and a few minutes later they ran into snow squalls and air so choppy the Fairchild dropped as much as 600 feet with a single jolt. Turning back to the west, they beheld protruding from the ice a crescent of mountain peaks extending southward. Like Wilkins, Byrd was anxious to honor his backers and immediately christened this range the Rockefeller Mountains. Elated by his first long look at the Antarctic's immensity, Byrd returned to base.

It appeared that the poor ice conditions that had stymied Wilkins at Deception Island would not be a factor at Little America, but two days later a sudden breakup threatened to sink Byrd's hopes of reaching the Pole. The supply ships *Eleanor Bolling,* named after Byrd's mother, and the *City of New York* lay tied together in the shadow of the sheer, 60-foot-high ice cliff that marked the edge of the Ross Shelf. The summer warmth had made the ice unstable, and a portion that was being used as a dock, covered with crates of supplies including the center wing section of the Ford, cracked and split into several floes. A chunk holding the wing section began to tilt ominously as Byrd's men hastily laid planks between the floes and rushed to rescue the vital piece.

Late the next evening, with a roar like an artillery salvo, another segment of the cliff crashed to the deck of the *Eleanor Bolling.* The ship heeled halfway over; only the heavy hawsers tying her to the *City of New York* prevented her from capsizing. As the ice slid off the deck, the *Eleanor Bolling* righted herself. But in the meantime a mechanic had been hurled into the frigid sea—Byrd himself dived to the rescue—and one expedition scientist who had been standing on the ice when it gave way now dangled precariously over the water, clinging to a rope. "This kind of thing," a watching crewman remarked, "could discourage immigration down here." Incredibly, there were no injuries and no damage to the ships.

On February 18 Byrd sent both the Fairchild and the newly assembled Fokker aloft for another look at the intriguing country to the east. Byrd, riding with Balchen in the Fokker, was again balked by bad weather, but not before he had discovered that the Rockefeller Mountains included at least 25 peaks instead of the 14 he had estimated. Searching to the southeast he spotted the dim outline of more high land not shown on the charts. He promptly named this Marie Byrd Land for his wife, "the best sport and noblest person I know."

By the end of summer, Little America was essentially complete, and the long Antarctic winter began to close in. The supply ships retreated north before the rapidly closing ice pack could lock them in. Forty-two of the men—the pilots, mechanics, sled drivers, scientists and crewmen who had signed on for the duration—remained behind.

Although the prospects for flying grew dimmer daily as the weather worsened, Byrd reluctantly permitted Balchen and radioman Harold June to ferry geologist Lawrence Gould 200 miles southwest to the foot of the Rockefeller Mountains so that Gould could gather specimens. On

Minutes after a portion of the shelf broke away, meteorologist Henry Harrison clings to the rope that saved him, while his rescuer reaches toward him. A quick-thinking colleague had thrown him a second rope, with a loop in it, into which Harrison slipped his boot—lessening the strain on his hands.

March 7 the three took off in the Fokker, arrived at the site and set to work. Two days later, a blizzard struck. Its winds rocked the plane—tethered only by lines anchored in the snow—and lifted one wing high off the ground. The three men labored frantically to tie down the wings with more lines, piled snow on the skis to hold them in place and built a wall of snow blocks around the Fokker to shield it from the wind. Thinking the craft secure, they retreated to their tent and lay there listening to the gunfire-like snapping of its canvas in the wind; only the fact that the tent poles had frozen in the ice kept the shelter from blowing away. The gusts subsided a little during the next few days, but flying was out of the question.

On March 15, the gale returned in full force, raging more violently than before. All day long, the men battled to reinforce the wall around the Fokker while its propeller whirled as if in flight; the air-speed indicator on the Fokker's instrument panel showed a wind velocity of 100 miles an hour. Hanging onto a line, June glanced up to see Gould clinging to another line with his body stretched taut and parallel to the ground like a flag.

By the time the men crawled exhausted into their wet sleeping bags, the wind was blowing even harder and they had to shout to one another above its shrieks. About midnight, Balchen, lying in the tent, heard it reach a crescendo of fury. The blast began as "a far-off moaning, building up to a roar like an approaching express train down the mountain and across the snow toward us." There was a boom, and then silence. They peered out of the tent. The Fokker had been lifted by the wind, carried backward for about half a mile and smashed into the ice.

The brawny Balchen insisted on making a personal inspection of the plane. With the wind behind him, he reached it in what looked like three long strides, then crawled back on his hands and knees to report that it was finished. The propeller and undercarriage had been damaged beyond repair.

There was nothing to do but wait for rescue. Having moved the radio receiver to the tent, they could hear the increasingly anxious calls from Byrd at Little America, but they were unable to reply—their transmitter, too difficult to disassemble, had been left in the Fokker and it was ruined.

Alarmed, Byrd was determined to go in search of his missing men, and on March 19, clear weather permitted him to take to the air with pilot Dean Smith—a veteran of the U.S. Air Mail Service—and radio operator Malcolm Hanson. They flew along the edges of the mountains until they spotted a smudge fire and a "T" made from orange flags that the little party used to mark its position. Landing at the camp, a white-faced Byrd leaped from the plane and dropped to his knees in a prayer of thanks. Then he sent Balchen and June back to Little America with Smith—the Fairchild could not carry six men—while he stayed behind with Gould and Hanson.

Yet another storm kept Smith from returning until March 22, when he arrived accompanied by June. Byrd, who considered the Fairchild crowded with only three men aboard, was concerned about its ability to carry five, but the pilot silenced him with a breezy greeting: "Hop in. Room for everyone on board. Next train leaves in six months."

With the successful completion of this first aerial rescue in the Antarctic, Byrd and his men suspended flying operations for the season. The two surviving planes were covered with tarpaulins and parked for the winter in snow-block hangars. On April 17, the sun flickered briefly over the horizon and then vanished, not to return until late August.

Byrd's fur-clad detachment stayed busy during the dismal, sunless months with scientific work and plans. They refined every detail of the polar flight and of the overland journeys that ground-support parties and Gould's geological teams would make in the spring. Between chores the men took what pleasure they could in the frozen world around them, observing the rainbow colors and dancing forms of the aurora australis—the southern lights—and investigating crevasses in the ice near the camp with the aid of searchlights.

Tireless and curious as ever, Byrd had himself lowered into a crevasse and found a glorious scene. "The beauty of that descent," he wrote, "I could not hope to describe. The beam from the searchlight fell on immense ice crystals, some of which were five or eight inches long, which festooned the walls and burned like myriads of gems. The walls themselves, when I glanced back, had by the light of the searchlight turned into emerald green and blue and seemed transparent."

Preparations gradually increased in intensity through October and early November. By mid-October, Byrd thought it safe to dispatch a sled party south to establish a fuel cache for his polar flight at the base of the Queen Maud Range, halfway between Little America and the 800-mile-distant Pole, but the still-appalling weather forced the men back after they deposited supplies only 100 miles out. Another ground party set off on October 15 with the purpose of establishing supply bases at 50-mile intervals along the geologist's planned route south to the foot of the Queen Maud Range.

In early November, Byrd heard that Wilkins had returned to Deception Island. Still eager to make the long flight from Graham Land to Byrd's camp, Wilkins had sailed from New York for Antarctica in September. He had told reporters before he left that he expected to have Christmas dinner with the commander. Byrd wired Wilkins that they would save him a penguin leg.

As it turned out, Wilkins was headed for another season of frustration and disappointment. He discovered that ice conditions on Deception Island were even worse than they had been the year before. Unable to find a good ice runway for his ski-equipped Vegas after several weeks of searching, he switched to pontoons but managed only a few relatively short flights because of the unrelentingly bad weather. He was further disheartened to learn that his comrade Ben Eielson, who had taken a lucrative aviation job in Alaska, had been killed while flying cargo from an ice-locked ship off the Siberian coast. Wilkins had no choice but to retreat from Antarctica once again.

At Little America, by contrast, things were going well. On November 13, Byrd test-flew the *Floyd Bennett* satisfactorily, having filled it with blocks of ice to simulate the load it would carry to the Pole. Then, impatient at delay, he decided to airlift fuel and supplies to the Queen Mauds, to augment those the sled parties would leave there.

Dean Smith, who would be at the controls for this flight, confessed to a mounting edginess about it. He could not shake "an illogical expectancy that it would in some venturous way be different 'down there,' so near to the end of south." Stifling his misgivings, he lifted the heavily loaded plane into a clear sky on the morning of November 18 and headed south. Byrd was serving as navigator, June as radio operator and the photographer Ashley McKinley had been asked along to take pictures.

They followed the trail of the geological survey team, which had set out four days earlier, gazing down on dark, circular crevasses that looked to Byrd like "frozen whirlpools." Two hundred miles out, they spotted the dog teams laboring up a slope far short of the Queen Mauds. When a leak developed in the cockpit fuel pump, June was able to plug it with the materials at hand—chewing gum and tape. The fix worked, and the men turned back to the heady business of exploring.

They soon reached the Queen Mauds at the edge of the great polar plain, where they would establish their supply cache. Dean Smith— who described the mountains as "a dam holding back a lake of inland snow with a surface 10,000 feet high"—set the plane down on a pass-ably level patch of ice that looked to him like "furrowed flint." The party was 440 miles south of Little America, more than halfway to the Pole. Smith kept the engines running while the men unloaded fuel, oil and food, piled the supplies in a 10-foot-high mound and covered them with blocks of packed snow for protection against the wind.

Soon after they started back, June reported that they were running low on fuel; perhaps his hasty patch had not held. He dropped to 2,000 feet, reduced his speed and adjusted the fuel-air mixture that powered the three engines so that less fuel would be consumed. But the gauge reached zero when the *Floyd Bennett* was still 100 miles from home. Now the engines began to misfire; moments later, they quit. Smith dead-sticked down and bounced to a bumpy but other-wise painless landing.

While Smith and McKinley drained the oil from the engines into cans so that if it froze, it could be heated and liquefied, June attempted to raise Little America on the radio. He could get no response. The radio, which had functioned well until now, was dead. The transmitter had failed and the three men worked on it for three and one half hours to no avail. They were about to give up when they heard the unmistakable

The snowbound world of Little America

"That night the temperature dropped to −40° F. and from the bay came muffled explosions, the sound of ice contracting in the intense cold." Thus did Richard Byrd describe the onset of the fierce and sunless Antarctic winter in 1929 at Little America, the base camp for both his 1929 and 1933 expeditions. There, from mid-April to mid-August, Byrd and his men confronted two implacable foes: cold and boredom.

During the winter, Byrd's men seldom ventured out into temperatures that routinely reached −60° F. Instead, expedition members crowded together in 15 snow-buried buildings and traveled between them "like a family of moles," Byrd noted, in eight-foot-high tunnels.

Inside the claustrophobic world of Little America, the expedition members fought to avoid slipping into what Byrd called a "dull, stupid, dispirited monotony." Although reveille was not until 8 a.m., everybody thereafter followed a daily routine that, said Byrd, made it "impossible to eat, sleep, dawdle or work too much." Meteorologists and physicists conducted experiments while the rest of the men readied the expedition's gear for spring trips and flights.

When they were not working, the men kept busy with a variety of pastimes. They gambled for cigarettes, held boxing matches and took classes in geology and aviation at "Antarctica University." On weekends they listened to special radio broadcasts from the United States, watched films and staged shows of their own, which, noted Byrd, "made up in brawn what they lacked in pulchritude."

After a snowstorm, expedition members gather beneath Little America's only prominent landmarks—its three 70-foot radio towers.

Standing in a hatchway, a scientist tracks a balloon to gauge air currents.

Crewmen playing backgammon enjoy a broadcast from the U.S.

Hamming for the camera, expedition members pretend to bathe a comrade. It took so much fuel to heat water that baths were a rarity.

Nome, one of the sled dogs, warms its nose in its master's eider duck sleeping bag.

Bernt Balchen (left) and a colleague spar in the gym.

Seven expedition members wear dish-towel skirts, rope wigs and make-up for a production called the Antarctic Follies.

sound of an airplane engine and then spotted the orange and blue Fairchild. The always dependable Balchen had correctly interpreted their silence, calculated their position from early radio transmissions and set out to find them, bringing 100 gallons of fuel.

The Ford was tanked up, and Balchen headed back to base, expecting the other plane to follow, but Smith was unable to get the *Bennett's* engines to kick over. The weary crew spent the entire day working on the engines and transmitter. Again Balchen materialized out of the sky, this time with more fuel, oil and a booster magneto, which sparked the Ford's motors to life. When the plane finally arrived at Little America, the mechanics found that its troubles had been caused not by the leaking fuel pump but by the carburetor jets they had installed. The originals had been oversized and been replaced with smaller ones. But these were still too big and had fed fuel into the engine too quickly.

The commander did not let the incident deflect him from his goal, the flight to the Pole. Byrd took Balchen aside the next morning and told the Norwegian that he would be the pilot for the historic mission. June would be radio operator, and McKinley would take photographs; the inclusion of the photographer and his equipment would cost them perhaps 1,000 feet of altitude, but it would also provide a visual record of the flight and strong evidence to counter any doubters. The mechanics were already making a final check of the engines, the oversized carburetor jets had been replaced and everything else was ready. All that was needed was a clear sky and a favorable weather report from the geological party, still struggling across the ice about 300 miles south of camp.

The explorers planned to fly nonstop to the Pole and then refuel at the midway station en route home. Byrd knew that a dozen things could go wrong—"a flaw in a piece of steel, a bit of dirt in the fuel lines or carburetor jets, a few hours of strong head winds, fog or storm." The most critical test would be the high pass in the Queen Mauds between the shelf and the elevated polar plateau. If the plane ran into clouds there, it would have to turn back. On Thursday, November 28— Thanksgiving Day in the United States—the eagerly awaited weather report from the advance party finally arrived: The mountains were clear.

Balchen raced the gray plane down the hard-packed runway and nosed into the sky at 3:29 p.m. A half hour later the men gathered around a loudspeaker in Little America's mess hall heard June's first radio report—the explorers were 45 miles out, engines running smoothly. They passed over the 100-mile depot and then the whirlpool-like crevasses that Byrd had seen earlier. At 8:15 they flew over the waving sled crew, dipping low to drop them a load of supplies. The mountains loomed up directly in their path. June's radio messages, which had been coming at frequent intervals, now ceased, not to resume for another three and a half hours. Byrd and his crew were heading into their crucial confrontation with the Queen Mauds and June would be busy with other chores, including helping the photographer capture a visual record of the historic flight.

Byrd wraps a stone from Floyd Bennett's grave in a flag to take with him on his historic flight to the Pole and drop there. "It seemed fitting," he wrote, "that something connected with the spirit of this noble friend . . . should rest as long as stone endures at the bottom of the World."

As Balchen inched the fuel-heavy plane slowly upward he saw that they had a choice of two passes. One would take them over the Axel Heiberg Glacier at an elevation Amundsen had estimated to be 10,500 feet. The other, slightly to the east, crested an uncharted glacier and looked wider, as well as 1,000 feet lower. Balchen was trying hard to climb, but he had to fight for every foot. He and Byrd decided to steer the plane toward the second pass. June filled the tanks with extra fuel that had been stored in the cockpit and tossed the cans overboard to lighten the load. Cliffs crowded in on either side of the frozen waterfall of the glacier. The plane's altimeter gave the altitude as 9,600 feet. Byrd watched the nose as it bobbed up a few feet and then slid down again in the narrowing pass. There was not room enough to turn. They had reached their ceiling.

Balchen signaled frantically to drop weight. Byrd hesitated a moment, debating whether to sacrifice fuel or their emergency rations. The pilot signaled again, more urgently. "A bag of food overboard," Byrd ordered, and McKinley dropped a 125-pound sack through the plane's trap door. The *Bennett* trembled and climbed a few yards, but now they were in a downdraft. "More," Balchen yelled, and another bag tumbled down onto the glacier. Balchen edged the plane to the side of the gorge in search of an updraft that would boost them over, and all at once they felt themselves jerked upward and through the pass with about 500 feet to spare. Balchen let out a yell of triumph. The vast polar plateau stretched out before them to the horizon. Byrd could see the continuation of the Queen Maud Range angling off to the southeast, its spires glinting in the sunlight and tinted with subtle colors—"the most magnificent sight I have ever seen."

The Pole was now 300 miles dead ahead. Balchen maintained an altitude of 10,500 to 11,000 feet above a surface that alternated between smooth snow fields and jagged snow ridges formed by the winds. Byrd used a sun compass, supplemented by a drift indicator, to hold the plane on course, checking his drift readings against those taken by McKinley. June finally returned to his radio transmitter at midnight. "Flying well, motors fine," he reported. "About 90 miles from South Pole." A few minutes later Balchen spotted the first clouds they had seen during the flight. At 1:14 a.m., nine hours and 45 minutes after takeoff, the moment everyone had been waiting for arrived: The *Floyd Bennett* winged over the Pole.

Byrd directed the pilot to fly a broad circle around it to confirm their readings, just as he had done at the opposite end of the earth. Then he dropped an American flag attached to a stone from the grave of Floyd Bennett. This done, he composed a low-key radio message: "My calculations indicate that we have reached the vicinity of the South Pole. Flying high for a survey. The airplane is in good shape, crew all well. Will soon turn north"—a somewhat superfluous observation under the circumstances. His message was immediately relayed to New York and broadcast over loudspeakers in Times Square.

There was no jubilation aboard the plane. A complex man, Byrd had a flair for the dramatic and a keen understanding of the value of publicity, but he was disciplined and methodical and he retained a dry-eyed perspective in his moments of triumph. "One gets there," he wrote later, "and that is about all there is for the telling. It is the effort to get there that counts." Balchen, similarly unmoved, felt that their achievement was somehow hollow, "a symbol of man's vanity and intrusion on this eternal white world."

Now the challenge was to outrun the fast-moving storm clouds that threatened to close in ahead of them. A tail wind boosted their speed to more than 125 miles an hour and helped them reach the pass over the Axel Heiberg Glacier before the clouds did. They sailed over the glacier, and made an hour-long refueling stop at their cache at the foot of the mountains. Then they cakewalked home, arriving at 10:08 on the morning of November 29. The flight of 1,600 miles—almost precisely the same length as Byrd's round trip to the North Pole three years earlier—had taken 17 hours and 26 minutes' air time.

Back home in the United States the entire country, it seemed, joined in a cheer of jubilation. President Herbert Hoover cabled his congratulations and gratitude for this "proof that the spirit of adventure still lives." The *San Francisco Chronicle* echoed other papers in declaring that "a wonder-surfeited world can still feel a tremendous thrill" at Byrd's feat.

But at Little America it was business as usual as the expedition continued to make exploratory flights and began closing the camp. The summer breakup that would allow their ships to penetrate the ice came in late February of 1930, and in June, after sailing to New Zealand and through the Panama Canal, the expedition arrived in New York. The members were lionized; the ticker-tape parade in New York, witnessed by half a million people, was the city's biggest celebration since Lindbergh returned from flying the Atlantic alone in 1927. Byrd, accepting the homage with modesty and grace, said that the fact that pleased him the most was that the expedition had not lost a single man in Antarctica. He had, however, left his planes there, anchored on a windswept ridge; he had already made up his mind to return.

Byrd's problem in 1930 was finding backing for the million-dollar project he had in mind. The country was descending into the Depression, and it would take him three years to beg and borrow the necessary funds and gear. But by 1933, the much-honored explorer, now a rear admiral, was ready to go. He had a 115-man volunteer crew and two ships, the *Bear of Oakland* and the *Jacob Ruppert,* named after the owner of the New York Yankees, one of Byrd's benefactors. Unsure of the condition of the planes he had left at Little America, he carried four new aircraft—a Curtiss-Wright Condor, a twin-engined, long-range biplane that could perform on skis or floats; Fairchild Pilgrim and Fokker single-engined monoplanes; and, for short-range scouting, a Kellett K-4 autogiro, a rotary-winged precursor of the modern helicopter.

A fleet of limousines waits to convey Byrd and his comrades in triumph up New York's Broadway upon their arrival from Antarctica in June 1930.

But again there was a competitor on the southern horizon. Lincoln Ellsworth had embraced the idea of a trans-Antarctic flight, which Hubert Wilkins had been forced to abandon in 1930. Ellsworth's objective was nothing less than a 2,500-mile round-trip flight between Little America and the Weddell Sea on the other side of the continent, by which he hoped to determine whether Graham Land in the northwest and the Queen Mauds were connected by land beneath the ice. He had put together a brilliant team to accomplish his goal; he could afford the best, his wealthy father having died and left him the family fortune. The indefatigable Wilkins was expedition manager, and Bernt Balchen—happy to have work in these tough times—chief pilot. Their aircraft, the *Polar Star,* was a new low-winged, single-engined Northrop Gamma skiplane, with a powerful 600-horsepower Pratt & Whitney engine and a designed range of 7,000 miles. To Ellsworth the trans-Antarctic venture was "the only great pioneer flight left" in a world whose blank spots were disappearing too fast. His 16-man expedition sailed south from New Zealand in December 1933 aboard a ship Ellsworth had named for one of his heroes—the Wild West sheriff Wyatt Earp.

By January both explorers' ships were plowing toward Antarctica. It began to look as if the two men were engaged in an unseemly race to Little America, an impression that Byrd did not quite dispel when he said, "There will be no race, but we will get there first." The admiral launched his initial exploratory flights from open water while he was still well short of the shelf ice, but these forays in the float-mounted Condor were bedeviled by the ever-contrary weather. Byrd and pilot Harold June—who was as skilled a flier as he was a radio operator—barely found their way back to the ship on one two-and-one-half-hour trip after flying blind through heavy clouds and narrowly missing an iceberg. Another attempt was almost scuttled before it began. The two 90-pound sled dogs Byrd took with a sled in case of a forced landing broke out of their crates and wreaked havoc in the plane.

Ellsworth won the nonrace when the *Wyatt Earp* reached the shelf ice in the Bay of Whales on January 1 and tied up. Balchen and another expedition member skied over to have a look at Little America, spotting the snow-covered camp only when they saw a radio tower poking through the whiteness. Trailed by a flock of penguins, Balchen found buried in the snow the Ford he had flown across the mountains to the South Pole four years earlier, and dropped through the escape hatch into the pilot's seat while the memories rushed back. On the floor of the cockpit was the slide rule he had used for his calculations. Ellsworth radioed a message to Byrd reporting that the camp and airplanes appeared to be in good condition.

Eleven days later, after the Northrop was unloaded onto level, snow-covered ice next to the *Wyatt Earp,* Balchen and Ellsworth made a flawless 30-minute test flight. They were ready, Ellsworth said, "for the great attempt." But early the next morning, Ellsworth heard an ominous rumble. The ice on which the plane rested had buckled and cracked, shaken by a huge wave that Wilkins later said must have been caused by an earthquake. The sea, to his dismay, was now a "grinding mass of ice cakes and jagged floes." Crewmen scrambled overboard and rowed frantically to the small floe supporting the plane, but before they could reach it, the fuselage dropped into the water; only the wings remained clear of the churning sea. The men looped ropes around the craft and hauled it onto thick ice, but the damage—the skis were mangled and the spars of one wing broken—was irreparable; the plane would have to be rebuilt at the factory, 7,000 miles away in Los Angeles.

When word of the accident reached Byrd—who with his ships was hovering 100 miles out at the edge of the ice pack, looking for a way in—he at once radioed the offer of his Fokker. Ellsworth declined on the ground that it lacked the range for the flight he envisioned. Discouraged but vowing to try again, he ordered the *Wyatt Earp's* skipper to steam back to New Zealand for the trip home, leaving the field to Byrd.

The first of Byrd's ships to get through the ice, the *Jacob Ruppert,* tied up at the Ross Ice Shelf on January 17, only three days after Ellsworth decamped. The methodical Byrd, who would defer serious air operations until the following spring, set about making Little America operational. His plans included test-flying his fleet of planes and establishing a chain of supply bases for scientific ground parties, as well as setting up another advance base for meteorological observation 200 miles inland.

None of this was accomplished easily. On January 18, during the unloading, June and Byrd agreed that it would be easier to fly the Condor the eight miles to Little America than to tow it across the shelf. June fitted the plane with skis, and with copilot William H. Bowlin aboard took off from a section of ice in the bay. As June passed overhead, Byrd and the crew saw to their horror that the skis, instead of being horizontal, were slanting down at a 45-degree angle, making landing impossible. In their haste, the fliers had neglected to fasten the safety wires that held the skis in position. Bowlin tried to climb out on a wing to adjust them, but the blast of the slip stream forced him back inside. June's fine flying saved the precious plane: He brought the Condor down near the ice in a long, flat glide for landing, leveled off and jerked the nose up just before he touched down. The Condor stalled and struck the ice tail first, forcing the skis into the proper position, and the plane slid to a safe halt.

The Fokker fared less well. Taking off for a test flight in March, it hit a ridge and bounced into the air before reaching flight speed. The result was a stall and a crash that wrecked the craft. Two weeks later Byrd's Fairchild was forced down by fog while returning from a supply run to the sled party whose mission was to set up a weather station 123 miles south of camp. Byrd used the autogiro to locate the plane, much to the disgust of the stranded pilot, who scornfully described the rotary-winged craft as a "tired windmill" with no business in the air.

Nevertheless, by March the expedition was operating smoothly, the Southern Hemisphere's cold season was closing in and Byrd

was ready to begin what would be the most publicized and most perilous exploit of his second Antarctic expedition. He turned over the command of Little America to Dr. Thomas Poulter, chief of the expedition's scientists, and had himself deposited at the tiny advance weather station, where he would remain alone through the winter, taking daily meteorological readings. He reasoned that two men sentenced to such isolation would probably turn on each other, and that not enough supplies could be brought in to sustain three. The truth, as he wrote later, was that he was "interested in the experience for its own sake." The experience almost killed him.

Byrd professed to enjoy the first two months of his solitary vigil, but after that he began to feel progressively weaker. Eventually he realized that a poorly ventilated oil stove and the exhaust from his gasoline-powered generator were gradually poisoning him with carbon monoxide fumes. But if he turned off the stove he might freeze to death. At length his radio transmissions to the base became so feeble and jumbled that a three-man rescue party mushed off by dog sled to see what was wrong. Reaching his hut two days after starting out, the rescuers found their leader almost incoherent and so debilitated that he had to remain at the hut for another two months, cared for by the three-man crew.

When a still-weak Byrd at last returned to Little America in October, he learned that the expedition had lost another aircraft—the autogiro had crashed just after taking off in late September. Feeble though he still was, Byrd immediately began organizing a series of survey flights he hoped would clear up the major unanswered questions about the geography of Antarctica. Was there, as many believed, a long strait connecting the Ross and Weddell Seas? If such a strait existed, it would mean that Antarctica was not one continent but two. Did the mountains of Graham Land reach across Marie Byrd Land in a 2,000-mile-long cordillera extending to the Queen Maud Range? What were the contours of the coastline east of the Ross Sea and Little America? This project, though clearly less dramatic than a polar flight, was the expedition's main aeronautical business; it would begin in mid-November.

In the meantime, Ellsworth, Wilkins, Balchen and company had returned to Antarctica with a newly overhauled plane and a revised plan—they would take off from Deception Island and fly to Little America in several short hops. But Ellsworth's grand design was once again thwarted, this time by a combination of weather, mechanical failure and personality clashes. First, soft ice precluded a takeoff from his initial choice, Deception Island. Then a broken connecting rod necessitated a trip to Chile to get a new one—a delay that cost Ellsworth a month of

Lincoln Ellsworth (center) and fellow expedition members collect eggs at a penguin rookery on Dundee Island, their base in Antarctica. The eggs, said Ellsworth, "are delicious when made into omelets, but when boiled are like rubber balls."

valuable time. In December the expedition finally found a potential takeoff site on Snow Hill Island, east of Graham Land, but now an argument erupted between Ellsworth and Balchen. The pilot demanded that a third man be taken along in case they had to clear runways at their stopping points; Ellsworth insisted that the weight of an additional man would increase fuel consumption and thus reduce their range.

On December 30 the expedition meteorologist reported that the weather looked good for the trans-Antarctic flight, but Balchen disagreed and refused to fly. Not until the skies cleared four days later was he willing to chance it. He took off and flew down the coast of Graham Land while Ellsworth busied himself with his navigational calculations. Suddenly Ellsworth realized that they were flying north, back toward their base. "Bad weather," Balchen explained. Ellsworth peered out and saw a snow squall ahead, but it looked to him like "only a wisp of one with the glow of the sun showing on both sides." They landed at the base after only two and a half hours in the air. "Ellsworth can commit suicide if he likes," Balchen remarked to Wilkins, "but he can't take me with him." The pilot later told Wilkins privately that he had made up his mind not to risk the flight with only two aboard unless weather conditions were ideal. "There are some men who are born to champion lost causes," Ellsworth said, "and I am one, perhaps, for I shall not give up." But it was too late for another try that season.

Byrd meanwhile had embarked on a productive series of exploratory sorties during an eight-day period in November. In a 777-mile-long triangular flight over Marie Byrd Land on the 15th he surveyed 50,000 square miles of previously unexplored terrain and saw indications that a strait did not penetrate the mainland on the eastern shore of the Ross Ice Shelf. Passing the Rockefeller Mountains en route home, he spotted the Fokker that had been swept away by a gale on his first expedition, "frozen in a lake of green ice." Subsequent trips on the 18th and 22nd produced evidence that the Queen Mauds did not continue eastward but instead ended in a level plain 1,800 feet high.

On the 23rd Byrd and pilot Harold June probed beyond the inlet-like depression they had seen on the 15th and discovered a high plateau extending to the east. This suggested that Antarctica was a single land mass. The weather soon made further flying inadvisable, and the company sailed for the United States in February 1935, Byrd taking with him his surviving airplanes. But there was one major polar flight yet to be made, and there were still polar aviators determined to make it.

Lincoln Ellsworth and Hubert Wilkins, though defeated in their attempts at a transcontinental flight in Antarctica, had refused to give up. After two failures, Ellsworth was seething with frustration. Still anxious to add his own name to the short list of great Antarctic explorers, he was even more determined after a journalist suggested to him that he "try something different, something easier."

Disdaining this advice from what he called the "sensible, comfortable

Lincoln Ellsworth stands at "blizzard camp," where he and Herbert Hollick-Kenyon were grounded by a storm on their 1935 flight across Antarctica. In hopes of taking off, the two dug out their plane several times, but on each occasion, recurring snows and drifts buried it anew. Finally, after eight days, a lull gave them enough time to uncover the craft and escape.

world," Ellsworth mounted his third expedition. He chose the efficient Wilkins for his manager, and Wilkins found a new pilot, the Canadian Herbert Hollick-Kenyon. The *Polar Star* could easily accomplish their goal, the 2,500-mile flight across the Antarctic to the Ross Sea and Little America, where they could shelter. The party arrived in the *Wyatt Earp* on November 12, 1935, at Dundee Island off Graham Land, and by late November everything was in readiness—the airplane, the navigational charts, five weeks' rations for two men, a silk tent, reindeer sleeping bags, a collapsible sled, rope for climbing out of crevasses and a rescue plan that anticipated every contingency. Ellsworth estimated that the Northrop would average 155 miles an hour over the 2,200-mile route, which would get them to Little America in about 14 hours.

On November 20 Hollick-Kenyon eased the plane into the air and headed south with Ellsworth along the shore of Graham Land, but after only an hour and a half he noticed that the fuel-flow gauge was leaking and liable to burst at any moment. There was no choice but to turn back. The next day, with the gauge repaired, the men started out again. Seven hours of smooth flying brought them close to the southern extremity of Graham Land. Ellsworth was thrilled: There before him was a range of mountains no man had seen before. Jagged, rocky peaks pierced the clouds, extending as far ahead as he could see. He called this "the greatest hour of my life," and named the mountains the Eternity Range. But as Hollick-Kenyon jockeyed the plane over the peaks, he ran into clouds and violent winds that threatened to hurl the craft into a slope. Worried about the strain the storm had placed on their fuel supply, he swung the plane around and headed back toward base. Ellsworth, fearing that he was doomed to perpetual disappointment, argued heatedly in favor of landing on the nearby shelf ice to wait out the weather, but the pilot was adamant. They returned once more to Dundee Island.

When the next day dawned clear, they took off again. The weather remained calm and inviting as they flew down Graham Land and across the mountains to a high plateau beyond. Ellsworth named this new and unknown country James Ellsworth Land for his father. But now their radio faltered because a switch leading to the antenna was defective. A message received at the base camp when they were seven hours and 45 minutes out came in garbled: "Well. I estimate that we are at sevent . . . one . . . ereabouts . . . my guess is . . . at that . . . pect still clear . . . to s . . . ight dull . . . little no wind." A few minutes later the plane's radio conked out. "What shall we do?" Hollick-Kenyon asked Ellsworth in a note. "Keep on to eighty," Ellsworth replied, referring to the course for Little America.

Ellsworth found it difficult to navigate. The readings on his bubble sextant were erratic and unreliable, and he was unable to figure out why. Moreover, the white landscape was barren of any objects on which to take a drift sighting. Hollick-Kenyon passed him another note when they had been aloft about 13 hours. "I really have no idea where we are," it said, "but our courses carefully steered should put us close in."

He thought he saw a darkening on the horizon, which, in the polar regions, can indicate the presence of water. Perhaps they were approaching the Ross Sea. In fact they were only slightly more than halfway to their goal; they did not know it, but the plane was averaging not 155 miles an hour but only 100 because of head winds. An hour later, they encountered clouds that reduced visibility so much that they decided to land on the plateau, check their position as best they could with a sextant and wait for the weather to break.

Hollick-Kenyon set the skiplane down on the granular snow. Ellsworth's calculations provided the disappointing news that they were 670 miles from Byrd's deserted camp. At least, however, they had a reliable reading on where they were, or so they thought. They pitched a tent, had a meal and tried their emergency radio set, but they were unable to get through to Wilkins at Dundee Island. They knew their fuel might not last to Little America, yet they could only go on, since the fuel remaining would never get them back to Dundee Island. They took off again after a 19-hour respite, but more rough weather forced them down 30 minutes later.

Their uneasiness mounted over the three days that clouds kept them pinned to this site. Ellsworth was unable to get a proper fix on their position. The men had a hard time keeping their feet dry, and the moccasins Ellsworth wore under his boots began to shrink, pinching off the circulation. Ellsworth and Hollick-Kenyon finally took to the air on November 27. They were aloft only 50 minutes when a blizzard brought them down. The storm held them there for a week.

By now the long silence from Ellsworth and Hollick-Kenyon was generating apprehension at the Dundee Island base and in the United States. Wilkins, though suspecting that the trouble was nothing more than a defective radio, ordered the *Wyatt Earp* to deposit supplies at specified sites along the coast in accordance with the contingency plan. Russell Owen, the chronicler of the first Byrd expedition, speculated that Ellsworth might be at Little America already, "raging impotently" at a dead radio. The *Discovery II,* an Australian vessel that happened to be in the area, steamed south to lend assistance.

Back on the lonely Antarctic plateau, Hollick-Kenyon finally discovered the cause of their navigational distress—a screw on the bubble sextant had worked loose. A quick repair enabled the two to determine that they were 500 miles short of Little America. When the storm subsided, they spent the next two days digging the plane out of the snow, then waited through another day of wind before they could take off. Ellsworth was losing the feeling in his feet and losing patience with Hollick-Kenyon's stolid silence. The Canadian made a rare, unsolicited remark as they prepared to depart their cheerless camp. "Maybe this is all meant to try us out," he said.

Their trials finally seemed to be ending when they took off on December 4 and flew into a bright blue sky arching over a plain creased with crevasses. After three hours aloft they landed to check their position;

An exhausted Herbert Hollick-Kenyon rests atop the supply-laden sled that he and Lincoln Ellsworth pulled across ice and snow for seven days after their plane ran out of fuel. On December 15, 1935, the pair finally spotted Little America's radio masts, ending their 22-day Antarctic odyssey.

they were still 125 miles from the Ross Sea, and they had only an hour's fuel left. The next day they pressed on until they saw a darkening on the horizon. The Ross Sea, journey's end, lay just beneath it. But then their motor sputtered and died; they were out of fuel. They made a gentle landing. By Ellsworth's calculations they had only a four-mile hike to Little America, but without landmarks on the white expanse, they were soon floundering. They spent the next 10 days slogging through soft snow on snowshoes, towing a sled loaded with their gear as they searched for the elusive camp. On December 15 they finally arrived at the buried site, which was marked only by radio towers protruding from the snow and a few forlorn flags.

The huts still contained bunks, food, coal and even detective stories, and Ellsworth and his pilot settled in to wait for Wilkins, who was due to arrive at the end of January to pick them up in the *Wyatt Earp.* It was a long wait, especially for Ellsworth, who had left his glasses in the *Polar Star* and could not read, and whose feet had been frostbitten.

Uneasy partners from the beginning, the two began to chafe each other in their confined quarters as time dragged by—a week, then another, then a third. Ellsworth lay in his bunk, hour after hour, listening to Hollick-Kenyon in the bunk above as he turned the pages of innumerable detective stories, sucked on his pipe, which made a maddening gurgling noise, and crunched sugar candies. The taciturn pilot grew irritated as he watched Ellsworth use three matches to light his own pipe. "You must be president of a match factory," he snorted.

To signal their position, they had left an orange flag and a tent with a message inside near Byrd's old loading dock on the shelf ice. On January 14, Hollick-Kenyon returned from a trip to the flag waving a note that had been dropped from a de Havilland Gypsy Moth seaplane sent by the *Discovery II,* now anchored in the Bay of Whales. It announced that help was on the way. Hollick-Kenyon raced back to the site, told the rescuers who had arrived in the meantime where Ellsworth was, and the next day a party from the ship picked up the explorer.

Ellsworth, somewhat annoyed at being rescued by strangers instead of by Wilkins, was put to bed with a temperature of 102°. But with his great ambition achieved, he could now be offhanded about the ordeal it had entailed. He had made a spectacular flight across the continent, improbably surviving four landings on the treacherous ice and the bad guidance of malfunctioning navigational equipment. "At last the trans-Antarctic flight has been accomplished," he wrote from the *Discovery II,* "but not without some difficulty."

Antarctica, though scarcely conquered, had at least been probed and measured and admired by brave men in flying machines, men to whom the frosty expanses at the ends of the earth were the sum of all ambition. Ellsworth, one of the last of the breed, probably expressed the true feelings of these explorers when he quoted the lines of a poet of the day: "Who has known heights and depths shall not again know peace, for he who has trodden stars seeks peace no more."

~~

Documenting the wonders of Antarctica

"The aerial camera records much more faithfully than the eye and retains much more surely than human memory," noted Captain Ashley C. McKinley, chief photographer on Byrd's 1928-1930 expedition to Antarctica. But the pictures on these and the following pages, like the more than 1,600 others McKinley took—each with a 60 per cent overlap to provide a continuous record of 150,000 square miles of terrain—owed as much to the photographer's perseverance as to the camera's objective lens.

During the course of the expedition, McKinley documented the existence of mountains, glaciers and vast plateaus new to the geographers. Yet on each flight he suffered misgivings: "I dreaded the thought of returning with a weirdly disfigured film, a partial record of the trip, or, even worse, nothing recorded at all."

A different ordeal awaited him at Little America, where the film was processed. Before work could begin, tank, water heater and sink had to be thawed out, and enough snow melted to provide the 200 gallons of water needed to develop one roll of film. When the day ended, the developer was poured into thermoses to keep it from freezing. "No photographers ever exercised such ingenuity or overcame such constant difficulties as ours," wrote Byrd.

Grasping his 50-pound Fairchild aerial mapping camera, Captain Ashley C. McKinley stands beside Byrd's Ford Trimotor at the start of the explorer's 1929 flight to the South Pole. The roll film he used to document the trip was more than 75 feet long and could record up to 110 exposures.

In one of McKinley's early photographs, Byrd's supply ship, the City of New York, lies moored to the Ross Ice Shelf.

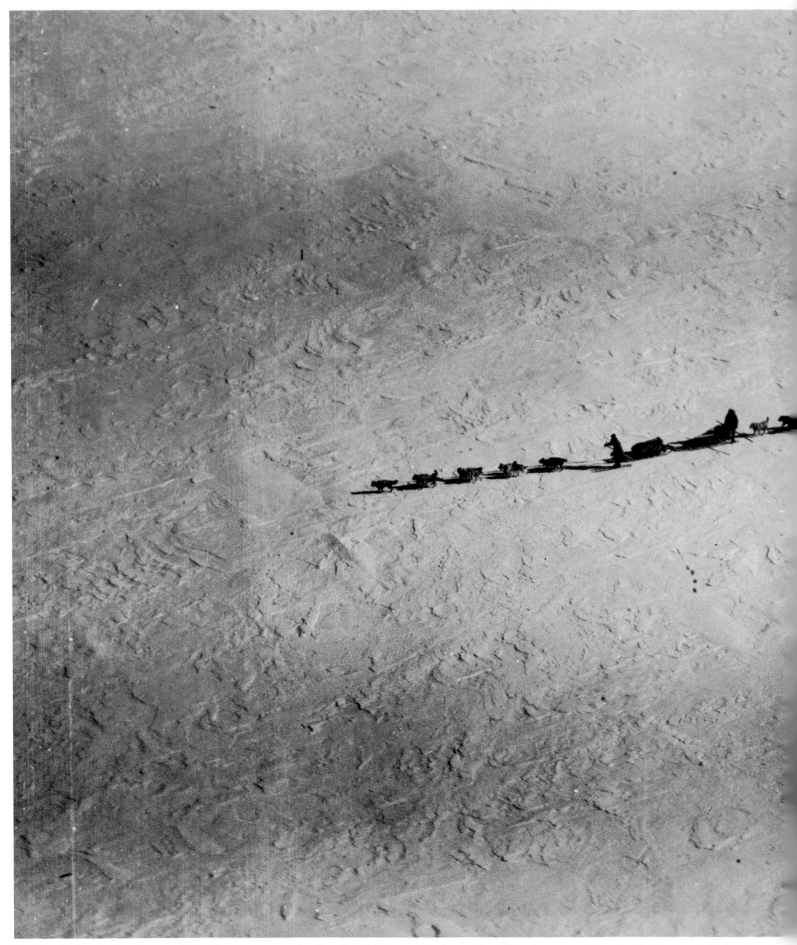

Two hundred miles from base, a sled party moves across the Ross Ice Shelf toward a site another 200 miles away, where it will set up a supply depot.

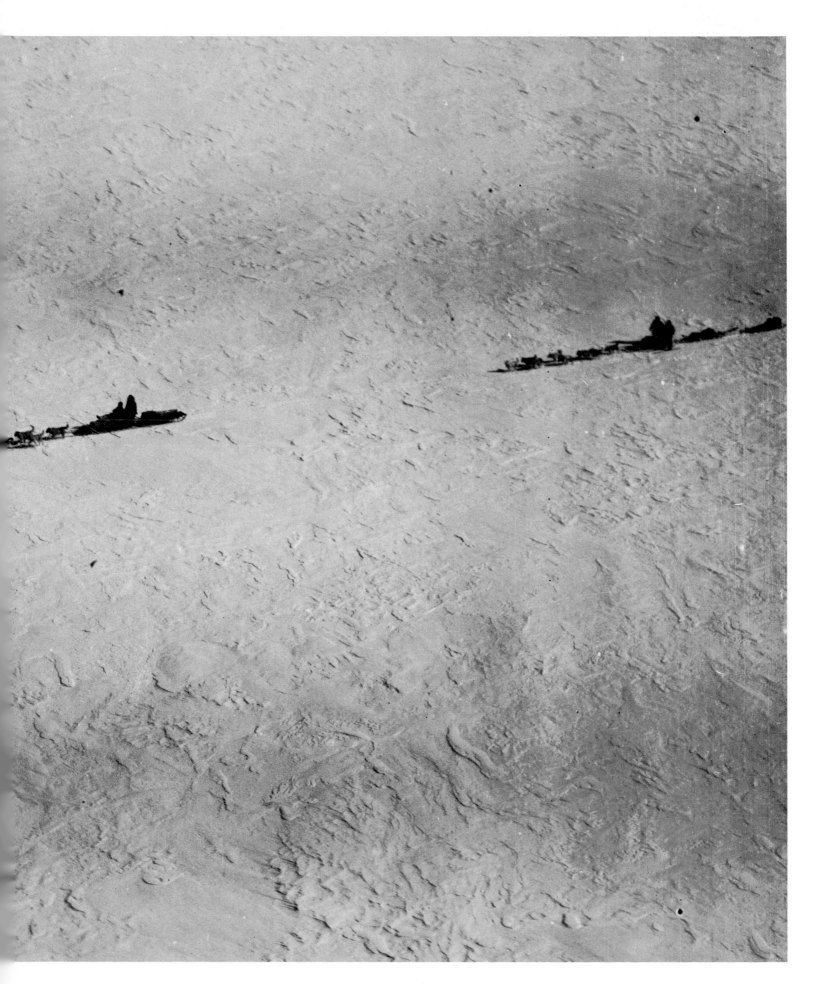

From an altitude of 4,000 feet, crevasses etching the Ross Ice Shelf appear no larger than ski tracks when in fact each is more than 20 feet wide.

Layers of snow in this low-level shot of a crevassed portion of the ice shelf conceal fissures extending to the sea beneath.

A huge ice island lined with crevasses sits grounded in the Ross Sea after splitting from the ice shelf during the spring thaw.

Returning from the Pole, Byrd's plane passes over the Axel Heiberg Glacier on the edge of the polar plateau. "Had we gone down in a tailspin, I am sure

that McKinley would have operated his camera all the way down," remarked Byrd of the indefatigable photographer.

4

The world's wildest yonders

The British, in the days of Empire, had long dreamed of a north-south corridor through Africa that from beginning to end would cross British-controlled territory. The dream came true in December 1919 when, after a year-long effort, the Royal Air Force completed a chain of 21 landing fields, stretching more than 5,000 miles from the British protectorate of Egypt to the Dominion of South Africa. In so doing, the RAF helped open up deepest Africa to aerial exploration. But the pioneering flights into the Unknown Continent were still fraught with peril and subject to bitter disappointment.

Within a couple of months four enthusiastic two-man crews attempted to fly the trans-Africa air route. Two of the four crews failed to get more than a few hundred miles from Cairo before wrecking their machines, while a third crashed in Tanganyika. The fourth—two Royal Air Force aviators from South Africa, Lieutenant Colonel Pierre van Ryneveld and Lieutenant Christopher Quintin Brand—demolished their plane in a crash on the Upper Nile, returned to Cairo for a replacement aircraft and started once more. This time they reached Southern Rhodesia before crashing—again, luckily, without any serious injury to themselves. There they waited for almost two weeks while a third plane was shipped to them from South Africa, and in that aircraft they finally completed their journey to Cape Town.

Regular air traffic in Africa was obviously an idea whose time had not yet come. A March 1920 article about the flights in the American Geographical Society's *Geographical Review* carefully delineated the obstacles Africa posed to aviation. Meteorologically, the article pointed out, Africa was characterized by fierce winds, ferocious storms, dense cloud banks in the mountains, mist in the lowlands and, near the Equator, "heat gusts"—vertical columns of hot, swirling air that could rise without warning as high as 3,000 feet and carry an airplane up with them. The thin, hot air in the central highlands reduced the lifting ability of the wings, made takeoffs tricky and taxed an aircraft engine so severely that "it may give out just at the most critical moment." If an airplane was forced off the carefully laid-out route—as might happen, considering the capricious weather—an emergency landing in unknown territory

Women and children of the Turkana tribe welcome Martin and Osa Johnson to East Africa in 1933 with a ceremonial dance performed beside Osa's Ark, the explorers' zebra-striped Sikorsky S-38.

would probably be disastrous: "A landing ground, in the ordinary meaning of the word, does not exist," continued the *Geographical Review*, and "even the most seductive grassy glades are pitted with termite heaps"—obstructions that could wreck a plane. A pilot who survived such a landing could look forward to trekking across country that was either waterless or "infested with lions, buffaloes and rhinos."

This dispiriting catalogue of dangers fitted the contemporary picture not only of Africa but also of the unexplored territory of the far Pacific and South America. Most Europeans and Americans of the time saw the equatorial lands as dark and mysterious realms of vaguely perceived terrors—of snake-infested jungles, man-eating animals and savage, warlike tribes. And the popular images were close to the truth. The tropical regions remained unexplored not because no one had tried, but because the hinterlands presented impassable obstacles to land or water travel. Men in airplanes, however, could do the job, and the adventurers of the 1920s and 1930s were quick to see the virtues of flying machines. As Albert Stevens, who explored the Amazon in the 1920s in a floatplane, wrote, "Where the untrodden jungle presented a matted and almost impenetrable wall to men on foot, it surrendered its secrets readily to men in the sky. The hostile Indians who had hindered previous expeditions could not obstruct a plane flying 3,000 feet above them, and no ground scout, however skillful, could match an aviator in ferreting out the easiest trails to be followed and forewarning of obstacles to be met and overcome." His airplane, Stevens said, served as the eyes of his expedition.

The motives of these aerial explorers varied. Some, such as Britain's Alan Cobham—who would attack the Cairo-to-Cape Town route—were trailblazers seeking to open the way for air commerce. Others, such as the Swiss Walter Mittelholzer, were aerial geographers who aspired to see and chart new country—in his case the most inaccessible reaches of Central Africa. Americans Hans Hoyte and Russell Rogers, who were among the first pilots to penetrate the back country of New Guinea, were serving as aerial scouts for teams of scientists; the Italian Francesco de Pinedo, the first aviator to fly across the Mato Grosso (Great Woods) of Brazil, was an airborne propagandist for his country, while the Americans Martin and Osa Johnson were film makers and writers who specialized in exotic locales and peoples. What they all had in common was the will and the ability to fly to the earth's wildest yonders and back, and to return not only with thrilling tales but with important scientific and geographic data as well.

Africa was the first and greatest challenge, and if anyone was ideally suited to explore the Dark Continent it was Alan Cobham. A former military pilot who had barnstormed the British countryside after World War I, the slight and mustachioed Cobham was part promoter and part aeronautical missionary; he was fired by a desire to show his countrymen that flying was both safe and potentially profitable. In pursuit of this

goal he had already made several trips into North Africa, and had logged an impressive 7,400-mile flight from London to Rangoon, Burma, in a single-engined de Havilland 50 biplane. By 1925, when he announced that he would fly the same plane the length of Africa, he was, at 31 years of age, perhaps the best-known aviator in Britain.

The idea behind the flight, which was financed by a number of British firms involved in the aircraft industry as well as by a film company, was to survey potential commercial routes for the government-funded Imperial Airways. The only major change Cobham made in his sturdy de Havilland, which had a range of 660 miles, was to replace its 230-horsepower Puma engine with a 385-horsepower Jaguar—the better to get airborne from the high altitude of the East African plateau. The route would be the same as the one his beleaguered predecessors had attempted in 1920—up the Nile through Egypt and the Sudan, across the high country and the great lakes of Uganda and Tanganyika, and on south through Rhodesia to Johannesburg and Cape Town. Equipped with everything from guns and emergency rations to "a light alpaca dinner jacket and evening accessories," Cobham, his engineer and the film company's photographer climbed into the mist over London on November 16, 1925, and headed for Cairo via Paris, Pisa and Athens.

For a brief while it seemed that Cobham and his crew might not even reach Africa. Before crossing the Mediterranean they made an alarming discovery. Cobham had ordered the plane fitted with low-compression pistons to cope with the low-grade fuel he knew he would have to use. The pistons he got were a mismatched set and were now disintegrating and threatening to destroy the engine. This near disaster caused a two-week delay while a special set was fashioned in England and shipped to Cobham at Athens. From there he made the hop to Cairo, and by late December the de Havilland was cruising over the White Nile in the Sudan and approaching the central highlands of East Africa.

Cobham, while serious and methodical in his role as an aerial pathfinder, approached the film-making side of his expedition with an insouciance that amounted to irresponsibility. At the Nile River town of Malakal in the Sudan, where the de Havilland landed on December 28, the presence of a band of Shilluk tribesmen suggested sensational cinematic possibilities to Cobham and the cameraman, B.W.G. Emmott. The tribesmen were instructed to form two groups, one of which would pretend to attack the parked plane with spears while the others defended it and the movie camera rolled. The only trouble was that the actors showed up naked, causing the film makers to fear offending the sensibilities of their audience back home. When Cobham asked the Africans to cover themselves, they obliged as best they could with hats, beads and ribbons. But as it turned out, explained Cobham: "None of them did quite what we had in mind, and this part of the film needed careful editing."

South of the Sudan the aviators began the long, steady climb toward Lake Victoria and the Ugandan highlands, the region where they expected the most difficult flying conditions. However, as Cobham dropped down to land on the 4,000-foot-high field at Jinja, on the north shore of Lake Victoria, he became aware of a totally unexpected hazard: Dozens of Africans obviously unfamiliar with this strange winged creature were running across the landing strip. Cobham instinctively cut the throttle in order to land short of them, forgetting for the moment that high-altitude landings demanded maximum power. The plane stalled and dropped abruptly to the field from 10 feet up. Fortunately, the de Havilland's undercarriage withstood the punishment without suffering any damage.

Resuming his journey, Cobham skirted the northeastern shore of Lake Victoria, passed over a section of Kenya and made generally undisturbed progress down the thickly forested length of Tanganyika. The plane hummed along steadily and even the weather remained docile. When on the ground, Cobham spent much of his time discussing potential routes and airdromes with British colonial officials; he hoped to operate an African airline himself someday.

On January 29, as Cobham was approaching Livingstone, Northern Rhodesia, he spotted what looked like smoke from several fires. He soon realized that it was not smoke but clouds of spray from 350-foot-high Victoria Falls. He was dipping down over the steep gorge for a better look when his engine suddenly cut out, the first time it had done so since he left London. It quickly caught again, but continued to sput-

Egyptian girls (above, right) take shelter from the desert sun beneath the wing of Cobham's plane during a refueling stop near Luxor. In the Sudan (right) a playful youngster sits atop fuel tins, shipped from the British Petroleum Company refinery in Abadan, as Elliott fills the craft's tanks.

ter. Cobham and his engineer, A. B. Elliott, immediately understood what was happening: The heavy spray from the falls was being sucked through the engine's air intake and into the carburetor, where it contaminated the fuel mixture. Cobham gunned the engine to keep the fuel flowing and climbed as sharply as he could, leveling off only when he was within gliding distance of the landing field at Livingstone.

As it turned out, the unnerving misfires over the falls were the sole exception to an otherwise flawless performance by the D.H.50 and its Jaguar engine on the African odyssey. Cobham's final southerly lap took him over Southern Rhodesia and South Africa, where he touched down in Cape Town on February 17, 1926, ninety-three days after his departure from London.

Cobham paused for a week in Cape Town before setting off on the homeward journey. Following the same route he had taken south, he covered the 1,700 miles to N'dola, a settlement in Northern Rhodesia on the border of the Congo, in only three days, then lost a day to rain; 1,000 Africans were recruited to march back and forth on the N'dola airstrip to pack down the dirt and mud until the runway was firm enough for a takeoff. The Englishman raced on to the Sudan in another three days. North of Khartoum a blinding sandstorm produced the only nervous moments on the return trip: Cobham lost sight of the Nile, which defined his course. Dropping to 300 feet, he flew north over the desert until he spotted a dry stream bed that led him back to the river.

He landed in Cairo on March 7, nine and a half days after leaving Cape Town, and a week later he was back in London denying that he had done anything special. "I do not want you to think that the flight was very daring," he told his exuberant greeters. "The main thing was organization and tenacity. Apart from that it was an everyday affair"—precisely the message that his trip was intended to propagate. He hoped he had shown, he went on, that flying was "not a fool's game but a practical proposition."

Nine months after Cobham returned to England, the Swiss aviator, photographer and explorer Walter Mittelholzer set out to duplicate the feat of flying Africa's length, but in a seaplane rather than in a land-based aircraft. He wanted to show that an airplane—in this case a Dornier Merkur, with a single 500-horsepower BMW VI engine, twin floats and a range of more than 600 miles—could span the continent without the help of specially prepared landing fields. The plane was named the *Switzerland*. And Mittelholzer's motives were different from Cobham's. The Swiss explorer was less interested in the practical possibilities of aviation than in its potential as a passport to the unknown. Where Cobham sought a direct aerial highway, Mittelholzer preferred the side trips and their inevitable surprises. A veteran of several pioneering flights over the Alps, the Swiss adventurer had also explored the skies over the Norwegian Arctic and the deserts of the

Victoria Falls spills into a 350-foot chasm in one of the first aerial photographs of the cataract, taken from Alan Cobham's plane during his 1925-1926 London-to-Cape Town flight. Cobham's cameraman, B.W.G. Emmott, was so involved with filming the spectacular waterfall that he scarcely noticed when rising spray, sucked in by the engine's air intake, caused the craft to stall for several heart-stopping seconds.

Mideast. His main objective in Africa, he said, was "to further geographical and scientific knowledge."

He was accompanied by a copilot—H. V. Hartmann—and by a geologist and a travel writer. The need to stay close to water forced them to follow Cobham's route up the Nile for the first part of the voyage from Cairo. But from Malakal in the Sudan, where Cobham had staged the mock battle between groups of Africans, Mittelholzer detoured 60 miles southeast to Abwong to visit the Dinka, an isolated tribe famous for their great height. The Swiss aviator admired the Africans for their simple habits, including nudity. "The less clothes, the less of our so-called civilization, the cleaner and healthier in body and morals the natives were," he said. He was equally fascinated by the nature of the land itself, noting the transition from desert to savanna he saw while flying above the Upper Nile toward Uganda: "What were at first a few solitary clumps of meager, parched grass gradually spread as we progressed southward until there remained only occasional patches of bare sandy ground. These in turn disappeared, until we were over an entirely grassy landscape."

After a three-week delay to overhaul the engine at Jinja, Uganda, Mittelholzer flew into his first tropical thunderstorm as he headed out over Lake Victoria. The downpour was unlike anything he had experienced in temperate latitudes. The sky blackened, gusts heaved the plane from side to side, and water seeped in around the doors and sloshed on the cabin floor. Suddenly the clouds parted and the storm ended abruptly. Rainbows of a vividness Mittelholzer had never seen before appeared above the Dornier's wings. Crossing the shoreline and heading inland, the men flew over a village whose inhabitants rushed to their huts in terror at the sight of the plane. Mittelholzer returned to the lake and landed at a place called Kisumu.

Here the pilot decided to send the geologist and the writer to Cape Town by train—the plane needed to be as light as possible to get the lift required for the mountainous terrain ahead. Even without passengers aboard, the Dornier had a hard time lifting off from the lake. The air at 3,700 feet above sea level was thin, affecting the power of the engine. Mittelholzer and Hartmann had to wait for a breeze and taxi a mile across the water before the plane became airborne. They headed southwest to Lake Tanganyika, then north to the Congo village of Uvira, beside Lake Kivu, becoming the first men to fly over the volcanic peaks bordering the lake. When Mittelholzer visited Uvira, the villagers pointed at the sky and then at him, greeting him with cries of *"Bwana Ndege"*—"Lord Bird."

European friends had warned Mittelholzer and Hartmann that they would meet hostile savages on their journey and should arm themselves, but the fliers had declined to carry weapons. On at least one occasion their peaceful instincts turned out to be the right ones. They had taken off from a stream near Lake Nyasa and followed a course for the seaport of Beira in Mozambique, 450 miles away on the

Cobham (right) and Elliott (center) are greeted at Pretoria, South Africa, by Sir Pierre van Ryneveld during a stopover on their African flight. Van Ryneveld flew the length of Africa in 1920, but Cobham was the first to complete the round-trip journey, a total of more than 16,000 miles.

Indian Ocean. By 5 p.m. the men had been aloft for two hours and had already traversed a sweeping cross section of Africa's exotic panorama—great swamps, high plateaus flanked by mist-curtained mountains, a garden-like plain dotted with villages and finally the broad silver band of the Zambezi River flowing through its green valley.

Now, flying at 7,200 feet and by their calculations still 165 miles from the ocean, they had to decide whether to come down on the wide and beckoning Zambezi or gamble that they could make Beira before dark.

A nighttime landing in this daunting and sketchily charted country would be folly; the odds were that neither plane nor fliers would survive. Mittelholzer made a quick calculation: Three hours' worth of fuel remained; daylight should last for an hour and a half, maybe two; they were averaging 125 miles per hour—they would go for it.

Mittelholzer cast a wistful glance back at the Zambezi as they left the river weaving toward the horizon behind them. Below lay a thickly forested plateau, vividly green in the soft late-afternoon light. For an interminable hour they droned on toward the ocean, watching warily as shadows climbed the crater-crowned mountains rising from the plateau. Why could they not see the coast? They began to think that they had overestimated their stock of daylight and underestimated the speed of the tropical nightfall. If only there were a river in sight, or a lake. They changed course, turning away from the coast and toward the southwest, where their imperfect map showed a single river called the Pungwe. Could they land on it? They were still looking for it 35 minutes later when the sun set. Now they had to land on the river, and quickly; twilight is brief so close to the Equator, and night was fast overtaking them.

Mittelholzer, who was at the controls, finally spotted the narrow thread of the Pungwe winding through a steep-walled, tree-shrouded ravine. He dropped low for a look. Landing immediately was out of the question. All he could do was follow the river and hope that it widened while he could still see it. Even if he could find a place to set down, he knew, he would not necessarily be able to get up again. He needed a long, straight stretch of water for a takeoff run.

Desperate minutes passed as they flew on in the gathering darkness. Violet flames spurted from the exhaust pipes of the *Switzerland's* engine. The plane had no lighting, and Mittelholzer could see neither his instruments nor his map. Skimming low over the water, he at last spied a place where the river opened out and the bordering forest gave way to broad sandbanks. Unhesitatingly he swung around and glided down to a gratifyingly gentle landing at a point where the stream was about 60 feet wide from bank to bank. The Merkur skimmed across the water for a short distance and then smacked harmlessly into a sand bar.

The two airmen celebrated their deliverance with a dip in the river and a light meal before they draped their mosquito nets over the windows and settled down to sleep on the cockpit floor. Hartmann was already snoring half an hour later when five tribesmen emerged from the forest near the plane. Still awake, Mittelholzer heard the nocturnal visitors approaching and boldly climbed out to greet them. "Does one of these gentlemen speak English?" he asked politely. To his astonishment one man replied that he did, a claim that became even more remarkable when the African told Mittelholzer that the nearest village was six days' march from their destination, the coastal town of Beira. Soon after the bizarre geographical conference in the wilderness, the tribesmen departed. Mittelholzer crawled back onto his blanket.

But before he could drop off to sleep another group of Africans glided up in a lantern-lit canoe. Mittelholzer saw one of them staring at the letters spelling out the plane's name and writing in a notebook. This man, who also spoke English, turned out to be the village postmaster; he graciously asked the aviators if there was anything they needed. Mittelholzer declined with thanks and retired once again, but a short time later the first group of visitors returned, bearing two boiled fish and a half-dozen eggs on a dish. As far as Mittelholzer was concerned, this touching and unexpected display of hospitality proved the point he had made to his European friends: A peaceful explorer, he said, had no need of firearms.

Early the next morning Hartmann and Mittelholzer looked out their windows and saw what appeared to be the entire local population assembled in canoes around the plane. The Europeans took advantage of the handy manpower to muscle the Dornier off the sand bar, but their first takeoff attempt ended abruptly when the *Switzerland* struck a shoal. After tugging the seaplane free they tried again, but as they roared full throttle along the river Hartmann suddenly saw that three Africans were sitting on the plane's floats and clinging desperately to the struts. The pilot cut the motor and the outriders let go, falling head over heels into the water and swimming quickly to shore. Mittelholzer gave the *Switzerland* the throttle again, and this time the plane raced down the slender river for two thirds of a mile, then finally rose from the water, cleared the slopes of the ravine that enclosed it and climbed into the sky. Freed from the African bush, the aviators touched down in the bay at Beira 55 minutes later.

From there they hugged the coast of the Indian Ocean as they flew to Lourenço Marques, Durban and on to Cape Town, where Hartmann set the plane down near a pier crowded with cheering South Africans. The one-way journey from the Alps to the Cape of Good Hope showed that a seaplane could overcome the obstacles of African flying as efficiently as Cobham's landplane had.

Meanwhile, in the two years since his historic African flight, Cobham had flown from England to Australia and back home, there to collect a knighthood. Now he intended to head for Africa again with a larger plane and a plan to match. Still convinced of the feasibility of an African airline, he was determined to pilot a 10-ton Short S.5 Singapore I flying boat from Kent to Cairo and on to Cape Town, then return north along the West African coast. The Singapore I was driven by two

The routes of three pioneering trans-African flights are shown here: Alan Cobham's 1925-1926 flight from London to Cairo, down to Cape Town and then home again along a similar course (blue); Walter Mittelholzer's 1927 journey by seaplane from Zurich to Cape Town (purple); and Cobham's 1928 flight from Kent, England, to Cape Town and his return trip up the coast of West Africa (red).

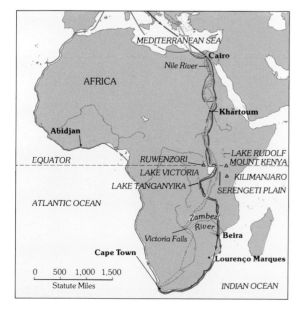

700-horsepower Rolls-Royce engines located above and slightly behind the plane's open cockpit. Joining him as crew were a copilot, H. V.
Worrall; a photographer, C. R. Bonnett; two engineers; and Cobham's
wife, Gladys, a onetime show girl.

The first leg of the flight, the familiar route up the Nile and on to Lake
Victoria, was enlivened by an attempt to photograph a stampeding herd
of elephants in the swamps of the southern Sudan. Cobham banked the
big flying boat to keep the sun behind it so that Bonnett could get some
pictures. Bonnett, however, had not yet spotted the animals, and to
attract his attention copilot Worrall stood up and stuck out his arm,
pointing wildly—forgetting that a propeller was whirling just behind the
cockpit. The prop struck Worrall's finger and knocked him into his seat,
but luckily the blow was a glancing one, with no more serious effect than
some profuse bleeding.

At the Ugandan town of Entebbe on Lake Victoria, Cobham inter-
rupted his journey. He backtracked the 1,350 miles to Khartoum to
make a survey flight for the British Colonial Office, an out-of-the-way
mission he agreed to in exchange for government support of the African
airline he planned. He returned to Entebbe and resumed his southerly

*Balancing on the wing of his Dornier
Merkur, Walter Mittelholzer greets boatloads
of well-wishers at Cape Town Bay, South
Africa, shortly after his record 100-
hour flight from Zurich in 1927. Looming
in the background is Cape Town's
famous landmark, Table Mountain.*

course, flying the Singapore I on to Lake Tanganyika and the Indian Ocean without incident along a route similar to Mittelholzer's. He touched down in Cape Town on March 30 and took off again a few days later for the trip up the Atlantic coast.

All went well until a storm forced the big aircraft down in a log-littered lagoon near Libreville, Gabon, almost at the Equator. Huge hailstones threatened to tear holes in the fabric-covered wings, and in the midst of the storm the tide receded and left the plane stuck in the mud. Lady Cobham, detecting the deepening gloom in the cockpit, dipped into the provisions and laid out an elaborate buffet featuring canned crayfish, chicken, cheese, biscuits and fruit. After this feast she grabbed her ukulele and led the crew in a round of comic songs while they waited out the storm. At length the weather brightened and the water climbed high enough to permit the refreshed and revivified flight crew to negotiate the debris in the lagoon and take off again.

They suffered the only serious mechanical breakdown of the trip while flying out of Abidjan in the Ivory Coast in mid-April. A vibration in the port engine compelled Cobham to set the plane down in a desolate lagoon near a French trading post, Fresco, where he discovered that the problem was a cracked crankcase. Repair was impossible; they needed a new engine. But to get one they had to send a message to the Rolls-Royce factory in England.

A French official helped the Cobhams arrange to go by canoe and motorboat up a river 120 miles to Grand Bassam, where they sent a cable and awaited delivery of the engine. Cobham waited for a month in Grand Bassam, and when the engine arrived, he had three canoes lashed together to float it back to the plane. Manned by 16 African paddlers, the makeshift barge glided along narrow jungle streams and through pools guarded by crocodiles. When night fell, the Cobhams could see almost nothing: Thick foliage blotted out moon and stars. The boatmen, however, kept right on paddling. "One native, who had done nothing all day, sat in the bow and looked ahead into the blackness," Cobham wrote. "He yelled orders to the man in the stern." The only sounds were "the shouts of the man with the cat's eyes, and panting breath as our crew paddled faster and faster into the darkness." At last they arrived back at the plane and in a day completed the exhausting job of removing the old engine and replacing it with the new one.

On May 15 the party took off for the last lap. Two weeks later, flying via Liberia, the Canary Islands, Morocco and Spain, they landed in England. In the end Cobham's bright dream of operating an African airline flickered and faded when he failed to get financial backing, but the idea survived, along with the route he pioneered: Imperial Airways began regular service between London and Lake Victoria in February 1931.

Even with a commercial airline operating on the Nile corridor it was possible to find plenty of adventure in Africa, especially for the fliers who went in search of it. Martin and Osa Johnson, an American

couple from Kansas, had already won a considerable following by writing books, making films and giving lectures about their travels; now they learned to fly so they could get a better view of the back country of Kenya and Tanganyika, which they had frequently explored in ground-based safaris. The Johnsons approached the wilds with a certain whimsical flair. Often accompanied by a pet gibbon they dubbed "Wah, the Flying Ape," they traveled in two Sikorsky amphibians. One was a single-engined S-39B that was named *Spirit of Africa* and was painted in giraffe-like spots. The other, called *Osa's Ark,* was a larger, twin-engined S-38C painted in zebra stripes. It was equipped with beds, a bathroom, and even a gas stove and oven, and was used for most of the Johnsons' aerial expeditions. Two pilots, a mechanic and three film technicians completed their crew.

By March of 1933, the Johnsons had established a comfortable base camp and a landing strip at the village of N'gronet, in a Kenya valley 175 miles from the Ethiopian border. One of the early objectives of their first aerial safari was 187-mile-long Lake Rudolph, a forbidding body of salt water on the border of Kenya and Ethiopia. Legend had it that the Omolo tribe, who inhabited an island in the lake, had once believed themselves to be the only people in existence, and the Johnsons were determined to visit them. But despite days of repeated efforts with *Osa's Ark,* they were unable to come down in the rough, wind-swept waters around the island. After a final try, they gave up and landed instead in a cove on the lake shore, and soon found themselves face to face with about 20 Turkana tribesmen, who wore their long hair piled high on their heads. Some of them adorned their faces with wooden disks dangling from their noses and stuck pieces of ivory through their lower lips.

The Turkana appeared to be more interested in the ornamental possibilities of the Johnsons' empty food cans than they were in the plane, even when pilot Vern Carstens took it up for a short spin to show off its paces. Though they almost certainly had never seen an airplane before, they were unimpressed by either the takeoff or the landing, but they did like the shade provided by the wings. Through an interpreter the Johnsons then persuaded several tribesmen to take a ride. Now, the visitors thought, they would see a reaction. But the Africans remained impassive as they flew over the lake's barren shores and a village nearby. Nothing appeared to surprise them. The interpreter pointed out a cow to one of the riders. "That is not a cow," the man replied after glancing down and observing the animals from this strange vantage point. "A cow has legs." The interpreter then indicated a tree, but again the African shook his head. "That is not a tree," he said with finality. "You look up to see a tree, and you can walk under a tree. That is not a tree."

Several weeks later the Johnsons moved their base camp and the *Ark* to the Serengeti Plain in Tanganyika, where they photographed lions, setting bait near the *Ark* to attract them. On one occasion Osa remained in the plane while Martin and his crew manned the cameras a short distance away. A male lion materialized, walked toward the plane and

An enthusiastic crowd waves farewell to Cobham and his wife, Gladys, as they fly over England's Medway River at the start of a 20,000-mile survey flight to South Africa in 1927. Cobham's 10-ton plane, the Singapore, was then the world's largest and fastest all-metal flying boat.

123

settled down to enjoy the bait. Disturbed by his growling, Osa leaned out of the open hatch and talked amiably to him, then noticed a look of alarm on her husband's face. She pulled the hatch shut just as the lion lunged heavily toward her. As the dazed animal withdrew she picked up the nearest weapon, a package of pancake flour, opened the hatch carefully and hurled it at him, powdering his mane and producing "a most satisfactory white cloud" on his nose.

The Johnsons' aerial meanderings eventually carried them over 60,000 miles of the African heartland, and they returned to the United States in the summer of 1934 with thousands of feet of documentary film. Even in the Depression, audiences readily paid to see the Johnsons' adventures on the movie screen.

Africa had been explored, laboriously by men on foot and more easily by aviators, and its wonders had been revealed even to people who never left home. But vast stretches of the New World, in the interior of South America, remained apparently impenetrable. What unknown tribes might live in its jungles? What ruins of ancient civilizations might lie hidden under the vegetation? What undiscovered animals and plants

Osa's Ark, Martin and Osa Johnson's twin-engined amphibian, wings over the giraffe-spotted Spirit of Africa at a campsite on the slopes of Mount Kenya. From this level clearing, the Johnsons made the first flight over Mount Kenya's 17,000-foot summit in 1933.

might be found? The ambitious expedition that Boston surgeon Alexander Hamilton Rice put together in 1924, for instance, was designed to resolve one of the continuing mysteries of South American geography: Precisely where were the headwaters of the Orinoco, one of the major rivers originating in the Amazon basin?

Rice thought he could reach the Orinoco's source by following three rivers through the jungles of northern Brazil: the Branco; its tributary, the Uraricoera; and that river's source, the Parima. He hoped also to find a mountain pass—described to him by Indians—that formed a land connection between the Parima and the Orinoco. Rice had failed in six previous attempts over 25 years to find the Orinoco's ultimate source in the steamy jungles of northwestern Brazil, but each time he had depended on water transport and had been stymied by almost impassable rapids. When his expedition of more than 100—explorers, scientists, aviators and the various crews needed to support the party—started upriver again in August 1924 he had a fresh ace in his deck. It was a small wooden biplane Curtiss Seagull flying boat powered by a Curtiss C6 160-horsepower engine and crewed by veteran Navy pilot Walter Hinton and Army aerial photographer and pilot Albert Stevens.

Martin Johnson demonstrates the wonders of his movie camera to an audience of East African Samburu tribesmen as Osa looks on. The camera, one of 20 still and movie cameras used on the Johnson expedition, was designed by Carl Akeley of the American Museum of Natural History.

A herd of wildebeest, frightened by the roar of the Johnson expedition aircraft overhead, stampedes across East Africa's Serengeti Plain.

While the main party traveled up the Amazon from the city of Manáos by steamer, Hinton and Stevens flew reconnaissance, scouting for Indian villages, establishing supply bases and mapping the river courses. The aircraft greatly simplified exploration: In 30 minutes, the flimsy-looking little Curtiss flew one stretch of rapids that took between eight and 16 days to negotiate by canoe.

In their reconnaissance flights Hinton and Stevens gazed down on light green palms sprinkled amid the deeper green of the jungle "like starfish at the bottom of an ocean." They discerned narrow streams—otherwise concealed beneath overhanging branches—by the steamy trails of vapor that rose above them. As the men flew farther upriver they sighted Indian villages set back from the water in concealment from enemy tribes. When they landed near one such settlement, the Indians rowed out to meet them carrying spears and bows and arrows; the airmen calmed the warriors with gifts of clothes and trinkets.

In January of 1925 the two fliers set the Seagull down on the Uraricoera River near the Venezuelan border to search out a site for a supply base. The boat bearing the main force of the expedition was perhaps a month's travel behind them. As Hinton taxied toward shore they heard the gut-wrenching sound of splintering wood. They had struck an underwater rock and damaged the hull. If the hull shipped too much water, they might not get airborne again. Without pausing to investigate, they took off, hoping to reach the safety of a settlement called Boa Esperança 150 miles downstream. But it was already late afternoon, and before long they were squinting into the gathering dusk and looking for a likely place to land on the river. Spotting an island bordered by a sand bar, Hinton touched down on the water and eased the flying boat onto the sand. The island was about a mile long and apparently uninhabited. They erected a tent and spent the next day patching the hull with canvas and strips of mahogany they carried with them for just such a purpose.

A new problem developed as they worked: The river dropped, no rain having fallen for several days, leaving the plane high and dry. Unable to move the aircraft without help, they settled in to wait for rain to swell the river, sustaining themselves on their emergency rations and an occasional fish. Two days later four Indians in a canoe paddled warily into view. The pilots, frightened but hospitable, shared their breakfast with the visitors. The Indians simply examined the plane without comment and glided off. Three days of rain finally resulted in a rise in the river, and on the 11th day after they landed Hinton and Stevens were able to take off and return to the expedition's floating headquarters. Twenty miles from Boa Esperança, their destination, they sighted—struggling through the rapids in canoes—the rescue party that had been dispatched to locate them.

By March Rice's band was closing in on their objective, and on March 11, Hinton and Stevens were able to make a four-hour flight up the canyon of the Parima River, satisfying themselves that no mountain pass connected it with the Orinoco. They were now traversing country that no explorer, airborne or otherwise, had ever seen before. The river foamed between jungle-clad hills beneath them. Waterfalls spilled down the slopes. Indian villages with large round-roofed huts squatted amid the trees. Hinton and Stevens dropped trinkets attached to small, homemade parachutes; these were meant as peace offerings to show the Indians that Rice's party, on its way to them, had friendly intentions.

Turning back when their fuel was half gone, they dipped low to photograph a village nestled in a canyon and then found that they could not climb out of the canyon; the air was so hot that the water in the radiator was boiling and the engine had lost much of its power. Hinton banked repeatedly to follow the narrow river between towering cliffs only a few yards away from the aircraft's wing tips. Fighting for every foot of altitude, he finally cleared the canyon. Beyond it, the river broadened out to a long smooth stretch he could use for landing.

With the completion of this flight, the main aerial work of the Rice expedition was done. Delighted with the crucial contribution made by his air arm, Rice went on by land and water to reach the headwaters of the Parima and complete the first accurate mapping of the Amazon's tributaries; the area of jungle he surveyed was 500,000 square miles, larger than France and Germany combined.

Some 500 miles south of the Amazon lay the impenetrable jungle called the Mato Grosso, a vast rain forest that spread across central Brazil. Like the region over which Hinton and Stevens had flown, the Mato Grosso was terra incognita. The best way to traverse it was in a plane that could alight on the narrow rivers. But the streams were frequently inaccessible or even invisible beneath the treetops that formed a great green umbrella. All of this made the region that much more fascinating to an Italian military aviator named Francesco de Pinedo, who arrived on its southern fringes in March of 1927 in a sleek, twin-engined, double-hulled Savoia-Marchetti S.55 flying boat.

The 37-year-old de Pinedo, accompanied by two crewmen, was flying a 60,000-mile, round-the-world good-will mission for his government. Premier Benito Mussolini had asked him to "carry Italy's greetings to the New World." De Pinedo's aircraft was named the *Santa Maria* to remind the Americas that Columbus, too, had been Italian.

On approaching the forbidding green tangle of the Mato Grosso, de Pinedo was startled to see what looked like several planes heading toward him. Seconds later he realized that it was a flock of large vultures. Fearing a collision, de Pinedo maneuvered frantically to elude them. He put the plane through a series of erratic banks and steep climbs and dives, but the birds continued to circle indifferently within a few yards of the machine. "One had lost patches of feathers," de Pinedo reported later. "Its bare thighs were big, fat and dimpled, like a baby's."

De Pinedo landed on the Paraguay River, at São Luis de Cáceres, to fuel, but now his problem was how to get back into the air. The river was so sinuous that he had to hire a boat to tow the *Santa Maria* to an

The routes of two daring aerial journeys into the virtually uncharted interior of South America are traced here. In 1924, the Alexander Hamilton Rice expedition undertook a 900-mile flight (blue line) from Manáos up the Negro and Branco Rivers to the headwaters of the Amazon. Three years later, Francesco de Pinedo flew across the dense Mato Grosso jungle (red line) from Asunción to São Luis de Cáceres, Brazil, then on to North America as part of a 60,000-mile globe-hopping jaunt.

appropriate takeoff point, which took three mosquito-bedeviled days to reach. Once in the air the aviator found himself over "solid, dense, dark green vegetation so unbroken that I had to steer my way across it by compass, as I did across the sea." Neither streams nor trails could be seen. As he headed for his next navigational checkpoint, the village of Mato Grosso, he ran into clouds and had to duck down until he was skimming the tops of the high trees in order to see the landmarks that he used to verify his course. He eventually spied the red roofs of the village and circled twice to give the inhabitants their first look at an airplane.

The clouds began to break up as de Pinedo searched for a river junction where his expedition's agents were supposed to have shipped a fuel supply, but when he reached it there was no sign of his cache. He checked the gauge and determined that he had enough fuel to get to the town of Guajará Mirim, 360 miles away on the Bolivian frontier. His course now took him along the Guaporé River, and from time to time he could see Indians, "their bronze bodies as motionless as statues," staring up at the plane. Nine hours after starting out, he completed the 360-mile run to Guajará Mirim, where he refueled.

On the next day, en route to Manáos, the city on the Amazon that the Rice expedition had used as a jumping-off point, he was forced down on the Madeira River by violent storms. As soon as they ended, he took off again in time to touch down at Manáos before nightfall. There the fliers led an impromptu parade to the cathedral, where the residents joined in prayers of thanksgiving. Back in the air a day later de Pinedo and his crew had cause to wonder if the prayers were premature: A torrential storm on the Amazon assailed them with rain so heavy that it sounded as if stones were crashing onto the plane. Slamming up and down in the wind, the Santa Maria finally made it through to Pará on the Atlantic coast and the end of one of the most daring excursions in aviation history. A quarter of a century later, in 1952, the crash of a Pan American Airways Boeing 377 Stratocruiser in the Mato Grosso showed just how daring the Italians' flight had been. It took 30 aircraft three days just to find the Stratocruiser's wreckage. When de Pinedo and his crew made their flight, there were no organized search-and-rescue facilities and there was only a handful of airplanes in all of Brazil.

Halfway across the world from the South American rain forest lay a Pacific island, richly endowed but so remote and so inimical in its terrain that information about it amounted to legend. The jungles of New Guinea were in many ways the least-known inhabited territory in the world in the 1920s and 1930s. The eastern half, known as Papua New Guinea, was governed by the British, and the western half by the Dutch, but in fact New Guinea was little influenced by its European masters. Crisscrossed by mountains and jungles where tribes lived a Stone Age existence, it had resisted the efforts of scientists and geographers to plumb its mysteries primarily because of its great distances and forbidding landscape—two obstacles that planes were uniquely qualified to overcome. The earliest explorations by air were made by members of a 1926 expedition cosponsored by the Dutch government and the Smithsonian Institution. The leader of the American contingent, a California ethnologist named Matthew Stirling, hoped to locate and describe the pygmy tribes that reportedly lived in the Nassau Mountains of Dutch New Guinea. He also intended to map their previously uncharted homeland.

The air support for this effort was a French-built Breguet seaplane with twin floats. The aircraft, a Br. 14 named the *Ern,* was powered by a single 400-horsepower Liberty engine and flown by Hans Hoyte, an American pilot of Dutch ancestry. Hoyte and his plane were supposed to reconnoiter the territory from the air and transport supplies to a series of camps on the way to the pygmies' domain. The expedition's 400 other members would follow by land and water. They were a varied and colorful lot, including 70 Dyak head-hunters recruited from the island of Borneo to serve as canoeists and bearers. For other bearers and servants there were 140 convicts chosen from Dutch colonial prisons. Almost all the convicts picked were murderers, because, Stirling said, murderers were "likely to be men of courage and character. Petty criminals and sneak thieves invariably are quitters, riff-raff."

On April 7, the first of the expedition's three ships left Java for the Mamberamo River on New Guinea's northern coast, to be followed in two weeks by the other two ships. Twenty-three days later it arrived at the Mamberamo's mouth and sailed 95 miles inland, as far as it could go. Base camp was set up there. On May 15, Stirling climbed into the Breguet's passenger seat, and he and Hoyte took off from the river for a survey flight with a cargo of supplies they intended to deposit at various points on the river and two of its tributaries. Hoyte struggled for 35 minutes to get the heavily loaded plane above the canyon walls that enfolded the Mamberamo. The aircraft finally emerged from the gorge and leveled off above a broad plateau patched and streaked with lakes and streams. This turned out to be only the prelude to a dramatic adventure that neither Hoyte nor Stirling would ever forget.

A hundred and fifty miles into the highlands Hoyte reported that they were running low on fuel and turned back toward the camp while Stirling looked for a place to land a load of supplies. They found a broad stream and came down, tying up at a low bank near a clearing. Stirling went ashore and immediately spotted fresh human footprints on the muddy bank.

The two men followed the tracks for several hundred yards into a dense tropical forest. They soon began to hear peculiar twittering calls, which gradually became louder and more numerous. Alarmed, they turned and rushed back to the plane, hurriedly unloading the supplies and stashing them in the nearby grass. The birdlike calls, growing louder, now seemed to be coming from all directions. "As if by some signal the bird calls became savage shouts and whoops," Stirling reported afterward. "About four hundred yards upstream six

canoes containing about thirty jet-black men appeared like magic. Downstream many more canoes and men appeared." As the canoes moved toward him Stirling could see that the occupants were fitting arrows to bows: "Hoyte jumped onto the wing to crank the motor while I cut loose the line and stood on shore holding the plane by hand. The first arrows slithered over our heads or swished into the river short of us. One arrow ripped through the plane's wing, and at the same instant the motor exhaust roared. With throttle wide open Hoyte headed the plane's nose toward midstream while I crawled along the wing back to the cockpit, our tail just clearing the tree. The Papuans, paralyzed by astonishment, stood like ebony statues in their canoes. Then they leaped into the river in panic."

Undeterred by this experience, Hoyte flew dozens of cargo missions as the ground parties worked their way upstream into the highlands during the next two months. Even after they had made peace with the foreigners, the Papuans near the base camp still loosed an occasional barrage of arrows at the plane as it took off or landed; one explained

Crewmen on a Dutch ship unload the Stirling New Guinea expedition's Breguet seaplane, the Ern, at the mouth of the Mamberamo River in May 1926. The plane was used for scouting and to carry supplies upriver to the expedition's base camps.

affably that they were "trying to kill the big bird with the terrible voice that frightens us." The plane eventually smashed a pontoon while landing in a storm and was no longer of use, but Stirling and his colleagues pressed on until they succeeded in finding the pygmies and mapping their mountain habitat. The little people, who stood not much more than four feet tall, turned out to be friendly and curious. The only time they became angry was when the explorers packed up to leave—keen traders, the tribe had found the intruders' visit quite lucrative.

The secrets buried in the New Guinea highlands continued to lure airborne scientists up to the eve of World War II. Among these was biologist Richard Archbold, who headed two successive teams from the American Museum of Natural History that penetrated the New Guinea wilds by air in 1936 and 1937, and again during 1938 and 1939. An aviator himself, Archbold, in 1936, recruited pilot Russell Rogers to fly a 760-horsepower Fairchild 91 amphibian on a series of personnel and supply airlifts to the museum expedition's chain of bases in the little-known Fly River country, a mountainous area in south-central Papua New Guinea. Set down on rivers throughout the region, the ground parties—and their enthusiastic Papuan helpers— fanned out to gather specimens of wild orchids, birds of paradise and other exotic flora and fauna.

But soon after it had deployed the last of the expedition's collecting parties, the plane was damaged beyond repair while moored in the harbor at the Papuan capital of Port Moresby on New Guinea's south coast. A leak in a wing-tip stabilizing float had caused the Fairchild to list. When a fierce storm, known locally as a *guba*, kicked up, it flipped the unbalanced craft over on its back, sinking it. The disheartened Archbold dropped supplies to his scattered troops with the help of a hastily chartered Ford Tri-motor to support them until they could be rescued by Papuan-built rafts. But the loss of the Fairchild forced him to reduce the scale of his expedition dramatically.

When he returned to New Guinea in June 1938, Archbold brought with him one of the largest aircraft yet seen in New Guinea. This behemoth was a 14-ton Consolidated PBY Catalina flying boat powered by two 1,000-horsepower Pratt & Whitney Twin Wasp radial engines, the same kind of craft the U.S. Navy would use for long-range reconnaissance and bombing missions during World War II. Archbold flew the plane out from San Diego via Hawaii and Wake Island. The Catalina, named *Guba* after the storm that had scuttled its predecessor, had a wingspan of 104 feet and a normal range in excess of 1,200 miles. Archbold obtained the cooperation of the Dutch government in organizing an exploratory journey into the harsh uplands near the Idenburg River in north-central Dutch New Guinea. Only two days after survey flights began, the aerial explorers made a breathtaking discovery.

Scouting for a ground route between the river and Lake Habbema, 60 miles to the southwest, they crested a ridge and suddenly beheld a

New Guinea's 40-mile-long Grand Valley, home to a then-unknown people, was discovered by Richard Archbold in 1938. It had 60,000 inhabitants.

large, heavily populated valley that had remained until that moment unknown to the outside world. It was filled with thatched-roof villages surrounded by walls and gardens, which reminded Archbold of the tidy farms of Central Europe. A network of branch valleys, all thickly populated, fed into the central basin, through which "a broad, braided stream" flowed. Archbold and Rogers made two more reconnaissance flights over the mountain-fringed Eden they named Grand Valley before selecting two landing sites—a lake and a lagoon on the Idenburg River—from which ground parties could reach the valley. Archbold's initial encounter with the residents of Grand Valley was friendly. Men and boys greeted his party with handshakes all around. The dignified inhabitants refused the explorers' gifts and stared as the white men swam in a stream, apparently amazed by their light skins.

The scientists discovered that the tribes of the valley had built a stunningly elaborate network of boundary fences and irrigation ditches using only primitive stone tools and sharpened sticks; their fields produced yams, taro, spinach, cucumbers and beans. Archbold and his men remained in Grand Valley for several months collecting biological specimens and trading with the inhabitants while the Catalina kept them stocked with provisions and supplied other camps in the adjoining mountains. Like the pygmies visited by the Stirling expedition, the people of the valley remained remarkably and sometimes excessively friendly—an annoyance Archbold found "far easier to contend with than hostility." The American and Dutch scientists finally took their leave in mid-1939. Most of them sailed for home, carrying more than 100,000 specimens and enough material for a blizzard of scientific papers.

Archbold and his flight crew, meanwhile, flew the Catalina back to the United States, taking the long way around. They island-hopped across the Indian Ocean to Mombasa, Kenya—the first time anyone had flown across the Indian Ocean rather than around it—on across Africa to Dakar, then over the Atlantic nonstop to the Virgin Islands and from there to New York, landing within a month of leaving New Guinea. Later they flew the Catalina across the continent to San Diego, just to complete the round-the-world journey, only the eighth ever to be made by an airplane.

Archbold's Grand Valley was not only the last great find in New Guinea; it was the world's last hidden area of major anthropological importance to yield to the relentless curiosity of 20th Century man. There might be small, isolated tribes still totally concealed from outsiders in remote reaches of Brazil's rain forest or the Philippine jungle, and certainly there were uninhabited stretches here and there around the globe that had not yet been explored, even from the air. But never again would an explorer find previously unknown peoples in significant numbers. The barriers that hid the last primitive societies had been breached in the only way possible—by bold aviators who in their powerful airplanes could go where no one had gone before.

135

Planes designed for distance and daring

"Across my distant vision flashed the most efficient-looking monoplane I had ever seen," wrote Hubert Wilkins in 1927. "To one who had been dreaming development of airplanes for 18 years, the sight of this machine was the materialization of a vision." Wilkins tracked down the sleek plane, a Lockheed Vega, and bought one to use on his 1928 flight over the Arctic.

The aerial explorers had to select planes very carefully. Those who dared to fly great distances nonstop always chose streamlined machines with fuselages and wings that could be crammed with extra fuel tanks. Richard Byrd used trimotors for both his polar sorties because they gave him a feeling of security—if one engine failed, there were still two more to get the craft home. Mountain fliers sought planes that combined powerful engines with great wing lift to provide reliable performance at high altitudes.

Some explorers picked their planes to reflect exigencies of climate and terrain. Roald Amundsen, for example, chose a Dornier-Wal *(below)* for his 1925 flight over the North Pole because its smooth hull did not have any projections that would flip the plane when it landed on snow or ice. Furthermore, its duralumin construction made it light enough to carry heavy loads of equipment and extra fuel in case of emergencies. And there was another advantage: "Aluminum does not break easily," noted Amundsen, who added that in the Dornier he felt "as safe as if I were only going to cross the waters of a fjord."

All the planes illustrated here and on the following pages are ones the explorers used on their expeditions and bear their individual markings and color schemes. The craft on facing pages are in scale, and the years in parentheses represent those when the models first entered service.

DORNIER-WAL (1922)
The back-to-back central mounting of two 360-hp Rolls-Royce Eagle IX engines on a 75-foot upper wing helped give this all-metal flying boat—used by Roald Amundsen in 1925—tremendous lifting power. The 7,260-pound Wal could take off carrying its own weight in supplies.

DE HAVILLAND 50J (1923)

To gain extra power for takeoffs from high-altitude African airfields on his 1925 London-Cape Town flight, Alan Cobham replaced the 230-hp water-cooled Siddeley Puma engine in his 50J with an air-cooled 385-hp Siddeley Jaguar.

FOKKER F.VIIA TRIMOTOR (1925)

Richard Byrd equipped this Fokker Trimotor with skis for his 1926 flight to the North Pole. The Fokker had three 200-hp Wright Whirlwind J-4 engines and a 1,500-mile range. It featured a closed cockpit and a double set of controls so the pilot could be relieved without inconvenience.

FORD 4-AT-B TRI-MOTOR (1926)
To make certain that he had enough power to crest a 10,500-foot mountain pass on his 1929 flight to the South Pole, Byrd replaced the 220-hp Wright Whirlwind J-5 engine in the nose of this Ford Tri-motor with a 525-hp Wright Cyclone.

LOCKHEED VEGA (1927)
Hubert Wilkins had the spruce-veneer shell of his Vega painted bright orange so it could be seen easily if he was forced down in the snow. He also had extra fuel tanks installed in the sleek monoplane, which was powered by a 220-hp Wright Whirlwind J-5 engine. The tanks more than doubled the plane's range, allowing Wilkins to make a 2,200-mile flight over the Arctic.

TARCTIC
TION

FLOYD BENNETT

NR-211

LOCKHEED SIRIUS (1929)
*Charles and Anne Lindbergh tailored this
trim two-seater, powered by a 600-hp
Wright Cyclone, for their 1931 New York-
Tokyo flight by adding internal fuel tanks to
the wings and pontoons. The additional
tanks gave the Sirius a range of 2,100 miles.*

CURTISS-WRIGHT CONDOR (1933)
*The workhorse of Byrd's 1933 Antarctic
expedition, the Condor was driven by
two 710-hp supercharged Wright Cyclone
engines. It is shown here with pontoons
for use as a seaplane, but could easily be
converted to operate from snow and ice
with the substitution of aluminum skis.*

WESTLAND P.V.3 (1932)
*The Westland biplane, one of two craft that
flew over Mount Everest in 1933, was an
experimental military plane whose broad
wings and supercharged 580-hp Bristol
Pegasus engine provided enough lift and
power to take it to 34,000 feet.*

SIKORSKY S-39B (1930)
This sturdy amphibian, painted with giraffe spots for Martin and Osa Johnson's 1933 African safari, was designed to carry sportsmen into inaccessible places. It seated five passengers, who had to enter through the hinged cabin roof.

NORTHROP GAMMA 2B (1932)
The ski-equipped Gamma that carried Lincoln Ellsworth across Antarctica in 1935 was one of the most advanced planes of its day. Its 600-hp Pratt & Whitney Wasp engine gave it a maximum speed of 230 mph; a 466-gallon fuel capacity provided a range of 7,000 miles; and wing flaps allowed it to land at less than 50 mph.

TUPOLEV ANT.25 (1935)
A streamlined 44-foot fuselage and a 112-foot wingspan enabled this Soviet ANT.25—called the Stalin Route—to soar on wind currents and thus conserve fuel on its 5,507-mile flight between Moscow and Vancouver, Washington, in 1937. It was powered by a 950-hp engine.

5

Vaulting the mountain barriers

My head begins to ache; I am shaken by waves of nausea; my breath comes in painful gasps; all the symptoms of seasickness and others besides. My voice is strained and distorted and, in an effort to make it carry in this thin air, I raise it to a blood-curdling shriek that startles me." So wrote U.S. Army Captain Albert W. Stevens of a critical moment on his 1930 survey flight over the 22,834-foot-high Argentinian peak known simply as Aconcagua—the loftiest summit in the Western Hemisphere. A veteran of South American flying, Stevens, who had been on the Alexander Hamilton Rice Amazon expedition of 1924, had not counted on his oxygen supply running out 500 feet above the peak. As soon as Stevens and his copilot—whose larger oxygen tank had not been depleted—began to descend in their Fairchild monoplane, his symptoms vanished. "How good the air feels at 19,000 feet," he exulted. "Seems like sea level by comparison with the air a mile above us."

Stevens' experience reflected but one of the daunting problems that high-mountain flying presented to the aerial explorers of the 1920s and 1930s. Pilots had to contend with freakish weather, particularly the winds that swept up and down and across the world's highest peaks; there was frequently no way for an aviator to know their velocity and direction until he was in their grip. The major obstacle to mountain flying, however, was the fact of altitude itself. An engine operating near sea level burns in its carburetor a balanced mixture of fuel and air, but one operating more than 10,000 feet above sea level must rely on air that is increasingly thin: The fuel mixture becomes unbalanced and the engine runs less and less efficiently and is increasingly hard pressed to power the plane. Some mountain explorers used aircraft whose engines were equipped with superchargers, devices that compress the air flowing into the carburetor. These had been developed as early as 1920, but they were still relatively new and untried. Many daring pilots simply depended on the strongest standard engines they could find.

A potentially more serious problem for fliers was that at altitudes above 10,000 feet, the oxygen available for breathing begins to decrease, and this produces reactions—as Stevens found out—that vary

An aide adjusts Lord Clydesdale's heated flying suit before Clydesdale and Lieutenant Colonel Stewart Blacker (right) climb into a Westland biplane in the first attempt to fly over Mount Everest.

with the physical condition of the flier and his acclimatization to high altitudes. "First, the hearing goes, and then black specks begin to float before the eyes and the sky appears dark and gloomy," observed Stevens. "At the same time the knees weaken, and a person, if standing, will collapse to the floor of the plane. If sitting, he will fall over in a faint. But if, just before passing out, he can force himself to breathe very deeply and get his lungs very full, he will gradually come out of his coma, even with a limited oxygen supply." Given some oxygen, the victim will feel his faculties return with startling vividness. "The motor, which has been silent, though running, suddenly bursts into a full-throated roar; the sky turns a beautiful dark blue; one can actually feel the strength flowing back into legs and arms."

Oxygen equipment had been in use by aeronauts since the 19th Century. The early devices were no more than mouthpieces attached by tubes to containers filled with the gas; these were later refined by the development of the oxygen mask in 1918. But tanks of compressed oxygen were not readily available in the far-off reaches of the highest unexplored ranges.

Another big obstacle to mountain flying, in fact, was the logistical difficulty that stemmed from the sheer remoteness of the most challenging peaks. The more accessible mountains that lay athwart the great avenues of commerce in Europe and North America—the Alps, the Rockies, the Pyrenees—were barriers to progress in an age of accelerating communications, and as such they were quickly conquered. What remained for the explorers were the farthest and highest, the massifs beyond the aerial highways and those too intimidating for commerce to challenge. A few were in South America and Africa, but the loftiest were in Asia, in the Himalayas.

The conquest of these peaks was an adventure with high risks, but it exerted an attraction that the men who patrolled the frontiers of aviation found irresistible. The satisfactions an airman derived from a flight over a forbidding range were in some ways akin to the rewards the mountaineer knows: the successful blend of flawless equipment and faultless execution, the brushes with the unexpected that quicken the blood and excite the mind.

For Walter Mittelholzer, the Swiss explorer-photographer who had been prominent among Africa's pioneering airmen, mountain flying came naturally. Mittelholzer had grown up in the thin air of the Alps, climbed many of the Alpine ramparts and developed a passion for flying over and amid them in virtually any weather. He learned to respect the fast-forming high-country storms and the fickleness of mountain winds while building a reputation as a skilled aviator and explorer.

Mittelholzer got a chance to test his skills outside Europe in 1930, on his second trip to Africa—and the test was a mountain several thousand feet higher than any of his Alpine challenges. The Swiss aviator had a strong, sturdy plane, a large, closed-cockpit Fokker transport

An ill-fated leap over the Alps

Pioneer aviator Georges Chavez clears the Alps' Simplon Pass in this contemporary illustration of his historic 1910 flight.

The flying machine that first vanquished the Alps in 1910 was a rudimentary, almost ludicrous craft compared with the planes that 23 years later would carry men over the Himalayas. But the Blériot XI used by Peruvian daredevil Georges Chavez to tackle the 6,600-foot heights between Brig, Switzerland, and Domodossola, Italy, was at the time the last word in aircraft design: a 462-pound monoplane with a 25-hp Anzani engine and a top speed of 40 mph.

Chavez completed the cold, gusty traverse in 42 minutes. But then triumph turned to tragedy. Coming in to land, Chavez blipped the throttle and pulled up at a steep angle. The stress was too great for the fragile craft; the wings collapsed and it plunged to earth, mortally injuring the heroic pilot. A journalist reporting on the flight said: "It is very probable that no one will attempt such a feat again." Yet three years later, another Peruvian, Jean Bielovucic, flew the same route in honor of Chavez' memory.

driven by three 200-horsepower Armstrong-Siddeley Lynx engines. The engines were not equipped with superchargers; even so, the aircraft had a normal ceiling of 15,000 feet. Proud of his Alpine conditioning, Mittelholzer carried no oxygen. His mountain hopping, however, was limited to whatever side trips he could squeeze in around the main business of the visit, in this case a big-game-hunting safari organized by the Austrian Baron Louis von Rothschild, a member of the European banking family and an avid sportsman.

As it happened, the safari's base camp on the Serengeti Plain was within range of Africa's loftiest eminence, 19,340-foot-high Kilimanjaro. No pilot had yet surmounted this twin-towered peak near the border of Kenya and Tanganyika, but Mittelholzer was sure his airplane could do it. He knew, thanks to recent discoveries made by sailplane pilots during experimental mountain flights in Europe, that the updrafts on Kilimanjaro's broad north face could help boost him over the top. Being the first to fly over Kilimanjaro would add to his already considerable fame, and he might be able to get exclusive aerial photographs as well. For Mittelholzer, the temptation was irresistible. Rothschild gave him the go-ahead to try it.

Climbing into a cloudless sky on the morning of January 8, 1930, Mittelholzer and fellow pilot Alfred Künzle soared over plains alive with zebra and antelope as they set their course for Kibo, the higher of the two volcanic cones that crown Kilimanjaro. The Fokker, stripped of its cabin furnishings and other nonessentials to reduce its weight and increase its ceiling, roared reassuringly as the outside temperature dropped from 72° at ground level to 44° at 13,000 feet and then to below freezing at 18,500 feet. As they neared the mountain, Künzle maneuvered the big Fokker along the north slope and probed for updrafts while Mittelholzer prepared to photograph the Kibo crater, which had never been seen from the air. Only by rising on updrafts could the plane get above 20,000 feet.

Künzle gradually edged the Fokker higher as he labored to control their climbing angle: Too steep a climb would reduce their air speed and bring them close to stalling. Despite his excellent physical condition, Mittelholzer was beginning to experience the headaches and shortness of breath that signal oxygen deprivation. As the plane topped 19,000 feet he could see the steep walls sloping down inside the Kibo crater. Forgetting his headache, Mittelholzer focused his lens on a remarkable scene: "The outer ring of the old extinct volcano was clearly outlined in sheer walls of ice and rock. The circle gradually deepened into a colossal arena at the bottom of which yawned a pit made by the last eruption of flame. It looked for all the world like the giant eye of some prehistoric monster"—a Cyclops eye a mile and a half wide on the roof of Africa.

They leveled off above the crater at 21,100 feet and circled it several times, bumping through the turbulence in a series of jolts. Signaling the pilot to turn back, Mittelholzer realized that Künzle was also feeling the effects of the rarefied air; his face was white and drawn and he com-

On their 1930 flight over Kilimanjaro, Walter Mittelholzer and Alfred Künzle spotted its peaks—Kibo and Mawenzi—minutes after taking off from Nairobi, 130 miles away.

Bucking high winds over Kibo's gaping crater, Künzle kept an altitude of 21,100 feet for half an hour while Mittelholzer filmed "what no human eye had ever seen."

As Künzle flew the Fokker Trimotor in great sweeps across Kilimanjaro, Mittelholzer photographed the three glaciers that spill 4,000 feet down Kibo's west flank.

plained of a fierce headache. Mittelholzer spelled him at the controls while Künzle retreated to the cabin to rest and recover. Over his shoulder, Mittelholzer watched the great mountain slowly vanish behind a snow cloud as they descended and headed for base and then, a few days later, home, to receive well-deserved applause from the European public for their bravery.

About 600 miles northwest of Kilimanjaro lay a compact chain of mountains that presented a different kind of obstacle to aviation. The remote and mysterious Ruwenzori range, which straddles the border between Uganda and the Congo (now Zaire), challenged airmen not so much because of its elevation—its highest peak measures 16,800 feet—but because of the rain and snow clouds that almost always shroud its slopes. As much as 100 inches of precipitation falls annually on the Ruwenzori's six peaks, earning the range its name, which means "rainy mountain" in a Bantu language of the area. Discovered and named in 1889 by the British explorer Sir Henry Stanley, the cloud-concealed Ruwenzori remained only partially mapped for decades. The mountains were still mysterious when American physician Richard Light and his wife, Mary, approached the range by air in 1937.

The Lights, who were making a leisurely round-Africa excursion that was part pleasure trip and part scientific expedition for the American Geographical Society, were traveling in a single-engined Bellanca with an enclosed cockpit, a supercharged 550-horsepower Pratt & Whitney Wasp engine, a range of 1,000 miles and a ceiling of 25,000 feet. The husband-and-wife team also had camera equipment and a familiarity with the photographic technique used in aerial mapping.

Dr. Light, a member of the faculty at Yale Medical School, was intrigued by these snowy peaks so close to the Equator. He and his wife planned a systematic series of flights that they hoped would lay bare the Ruwenzori's lingering secrets. Using a landing strip 90 miles away as a jumping-off point, they would begin by surveying the lower slopes and gradually move higher. Logistically they were more than ready for the adventure: They had oxygen, blind-flying instruments, parachutes, weapons and a medical kit equipped for anything up to and including an appendectomy. All they needed were a few nice days and a lot of patience.

They got their first tantalizing glimpse of the range from more than 100 miles away on a reconnaissance flight from Kampala, Uganda, on December 19, 1937. The sighting was just enough to whet their appetites. "I had been watching intently but saw nothing," Richard Light wrote, "then it was there, without question or doubt. Soft, faint, a dark quality of white, the summit of the range alone was visible as a mere deflection of the empty sky." Moments later a bank of clouds rolled up from the foothills and erased the vision.

By December 23 the Lights had settled at their camp at Mbarara,

Uganda, and were ready to reconnoiter the Ruwenzori's lower slopes, charting the identifiable features—villages, rivers, lakes—to an altitude of 9,000 feet, where clouds barred further exploration.

The data acquired on this flight enabled them to establish the base points for their photographic survey sorties over the higher country, which they began two days before Christmas. But when they reached an altitude of 13,000 feet on the first of these forays, they saw that the mountains were blocked by a wall of mist. On Christmas Eve they flew through a layer of storms to an altitude of 21,600 feet, but high clouds shadowed the few peaks they could see and sent them racing back to their base. They celebrated Christmas Day with two more attempts, only to be driven back both times by a dark shawl of mist over the mountains. A short-lived clearing the following day sent them up again with the same result. On the 27th a daylong storm pinned them to the ground.

The next day looked promising—hazy but not overcast. As he neared the range, Light was heartened to see a shaft of sunlight caressing the summit of the highest peak, but the Ruwenzori was still playing hide-and-seek. "Before our eyes a ghostly mist began to swallow up the entire range," he observed. "Clouds were not merely moving in, they were forming out of clear air along a wide front that made them seem to advance with the speed of an express train." Or a Bellanca. The doctor cast an apprehensive glance in the direction of his base and was dismayed to see a belt of clouds at 9,000 feet. Immediately turning for their camp, he nosed into the overcast and looked in vain for a familiar landmark as he broke out. He searched for about 10 minutes before the T-shaped airstrip finally appeared beneath the plane's wings.

The chronic frustrations were beginning to grind husband and wife down. Light was worried about their oxygen supply—they were running low and oxygen tanks were hard to find in East Africa. They could make one more try, but that was all.

The weather on the morning of December 29 seemed to offer some faint encouragement. It was foggy near the ground, but Light had noticed that low-level fog was often accompanied by clear patches on top. He taxied up and down the runway a few times to blow a path through the mist and ascended quickly into the clearest sky they had yet seen. As they climbed past 10,000 feet they were thrilled to realize that they had at last caught the Ruwenzori unawares; the entire range was visible. Light reached the ridge line and flew a zigzag course over the summits while his wife snapped pictures. The six great peaks, their white caps glowing in the morning sun, guarded a deep valley with an emerald lake in its center; other valleys fanned out from their flanks like spokes in a wheel. The Lights wanted to impress the scene on their memories, "to bring out to the full this miracle of snow on the Equator," before the mountains disappeared again. The bold, sharp peaks seemed a separate province, a 10-mile-long island of white in the middle of tropical Africa.

A glance at his oxygen gauge shattered Light's reverie. The needle indicator was dropping so rapidly that it was clear the tanks were leaking, and by the time the Lights finished their first roll of film the needle stood at zero. He decided to settle for a cruise along the east and west faces of the range at 15,000 feet. The flight was fascinating, for it showed how the chain progressed, said Richard Light, from "a mere wrinkle in the skin of the earth" to the rocky tors, "their bare sides gleaming like stalagmites in a cave." The Lights gazed enraptured at steep canyon walls that "rushed headlong together" to form the conical summit of Mount Stanley, the highest in the range.

But the cold and the lack of oxygen had exacted their toll. Light now noticed that his wife, who had been taking pictures through an open window, was blue with cold. A few minutes later she collapsed. He swung the plane around, descended and raced back to their base, where Mary Light spent three days in bed before she recovered.

The Lights, however, had successfully mapped the mist-shrouded

Richard and Mary Light (inset) made several unsuccessful attempts to photograph Mount Stanley, the highest peak in Africa's mist-shrouded Ruwenzori range. Finally, on December 29, 1937, they broke through the clouds and captured the "grim beauty" of the 16,800-foot mountain.

peaks: Africa's heights now lay revealed to Western eyes. But the mountains of Asia, thousands of miles away and higher than any in the world, were a far greater challenge.

As British Lieutenant Colonel Stewart Blacker, a veteran aviator, saw it, Everest was "nature's last stronghold" to be captured. Five and a half miles high and surrounded by huge chasms and menacing precipices, Everest was so intimidating that no European could get close enough even to survey it until the late 19th Century. In the early 20th Century, mountaineers began to attempt its brooding slopes; the most gallant of these, Britain's legendary George Herbert Mallory and his companion Andrew Irvine, disappeared in 1924 somewhere near the mountain's summit. No one, unless the dead mountain climbers had succeeded, had ever scaled the peak.

Blacker thought that a team of British pilots, flying British planes equipped with new British engines, could pull off aerial exploration's ultimate exploit—a flight over Everest's 29,028-foot-high crest. A properly trained and equipped expedition, he said in 1932, would not only conquer the highest peak in the world but also perform a valuable scientific service by conducting a photographic survey of Everest and its environs.

By late 1932, Blacker had sponsors for his expedition. The British Air Ministry, anxious to display British air power, provided one of his airplanes and other resources, as well as an overall commander for the expedition, Air Commodore Peregrine Fellowes. Crucial financial backing came from Lady Houston, a rich, eccentric and extremely patriotic Englishwoman who saw the attempt as a demonstration of British vigor and valor on the Indian subcontinent. The Maharajah of Nepal, whose country was normally closed to foreigners, consented to the British planes' flying over his lofty realm en route to the mountain.

The primary pilots would both be Scotsmen—the Marquess of Clydesdale and RAF Lieutenant David McIntyre. Clydesdale, a member of Parliament, explained to his constituents that the Everest mission was "the only original flight" left to aviation. "It is something big," he said, "and well worth while doing."

Fellowes and his crew had to prepare as best they could for both known and unknown hazards. To withstand the cold, thin air in their airplanes' open cockpits at altitudes as high as 34,000 feet, they would wear electrically heated flight suits and goggles. The oxygen for their masks would be funneled through heating units, thus keeping the masks clear of moisture and ice. A large mapping camera operated by an observer in each plane would provide the important strips of survey film, and the cameras, too, would be heated. One of the observers would also be assigned to shoot motion pictures during the flight, while the other would take panoramic photographs of the mountains; a film maker was on hand to produce a movie about the expedition. Weather information would be provided daily at the expedition's base in north-

Workers at the port of Karachi gingerly winch a crate containing one of two Westland biplanes from the hold of the S.S. Dalgoma. The aircraft were shipped disassembled from Britain for the aerial assault on Mount Everest.

east India. And the crucial machines for the flight were the best available—two single-engined military airplanes manufactured by Britain's Westland Aircraft Works and equipped with supercharged 580-horsepower Bristol Pegasus engines. One was referred to as the Wallace; the other, the *Houston-Westland,* or P.V.3, was named after the expedition's backer, with P.V. standing for Private Venture.

Fellowes tried to anticipate as many contingencies as possible before actual takeoff. "Do your thinking on the ground" was his advice to the pilots. No one knew the force of the wind currents that swirled around the pinnacle or precisely where a plane would encounter them. The crews would take no parachutes because of their weight, so they would have to fly out of whatever trouble they met. "We had not simply to know what to do," Clydesdale said, "but to be reasonably sure that we should do it almost automatically." The expedition members accordingly set up an elaborate system of tests, drills, checks and double-checks.

Pilots and observers—Blacker was to fly as observer in Clydesdale's plane and movie cameraman Sidney Bonnett in McIntyre's—tried out their masks in special RAF altitude chambers where the air pressure was

Pith-helmeted RAF mechanics work on a wingless Westland at the Karachi airfield. After the planes were reassembled, pilots test-flew them to 33,000 feet and pronounced them ready for the mountain's "turmoils and tantrums."

reduced until it duplicated that of the atmosphere at 39,000 feet. The all-important film was tested in refrigerated rooms to make sure that it would not crack at low temperatures. By December the two Westlands were outfitted and ready for their initial high-altitude flight tests, which the planes passed easily. The checking and double-checking continued until February 1933, when the Westlands were put aboard a ship for Karachi. Fellowes and most of his crew traveled to India by air, flying in three de Havilland Moths by way of Sicily, Cairo and Baghdad and arriving in Karachi in mid-March.

It was while flying from Karachi to their base in Purnea, near the Nepalese border in northeastern India, that they first caught sight of their goal. "Suddenly," Blacker wrote, "up from the hard, straight line where the haze met the azure basin of the sky, appeared three wondrous points of white." They were looking at three of the five highest mountains in the world—Everest, Kanchenjunga (28,208 feet) and Makalu (27,824). "Three immaculate snowy pinnacles swam majestically alone over this wine-dark sea of mist. We could scarcely bear to glide down to land and so lose the beauty of this sight."

The final countdown began in the last week of March. Further test flights at Karachi had shown that the planes and equipment were ready. At Purnea they went over everything again—the microphones for pilot-observer communication, the heated goggles, the connecting wires—and waited on the weather. Fellowes took his Moth up daily to check the cloud cover in the mountains that loomed 160 miles from the base camp; weather balloons gave them a wind-speed reading. Mount Everest's distinctive "plume," a streamer-like cloud of ice particles blowing east from the summit on windy days, was another tip-off of high winds. The expedition members soon perceived a frustrating pattern: When the peaks were clear, the wind was too strong to dare—a 40-mile-an-hour wind was as much as they thought they could risk. Higher winds would drive them off course, and by steering into the wind to counteract this, they risked using so much fuel that they would not be able to return to Purnea from the mountain. On the other hand, when the wind died down the clouds moved in.

Day after day the wind velocity at 30,000 feet and above remained too high for the Westlands to cope with—88 miles an hour on the 29th of March, 100 on the 30th and about the same on the 31st. The RAF ground crewmen the expedition had recruited in India kept the engines tuned. The pilots repeatedly worked out courses and estimated flying times and distances, groused about the demands of the film maker in their midst and converted a weed-choked riverbed into a swimming hole they shared with a crocodile, which they eventually shot. The wind finally lessened on April 2, but clouds persisted. The local astrologers told them that April 3 looked auspicious. The astrologers were right.

The weather balloon sent up at dawn on the 3rd showed a wind speed of 58 miles per hour at 30,000 feet—higher than their estimated maximum, but an improvement over the preceding days. Fellowes made a reconnaissance flight in his Moth, returning to report that he could not get above a high haze of brown dust that barred his view of the mountains. His engine had cut out twice at 17,000 feet, he said, preventing him from penetrating the haze. Despite the haze, the conditions seemed as promising as they were likely to get. The explorers decided to go and drove to the landing field at Lalbalu, 10 miles from Purnea.

The four who would attempt the Everest flight—Clydesdale and Blacker in the *Houston-Westland,* McIntyre and Bonnett following in the Wallace—struggled into their bulky flight suits and donned their cumbersome goggles and oxygen masks. At 8:25 in the morning they ascended into the haze and headed north over the broad plain that stretches to within a few miles of the Nepalese border and the olive-green foothills of the Himalayas. Blacker methodically ticked off the items on his checklist; all his equipment was in order except the interphone between pilot and observer, which was malfunctioning and could not be repaired. He would have to communicate with Clydesdale by notes. They passed over the airfield at Forbesganj, 46 miles from Purnea, which they had selected as an emergency landing site in the event they ran short of fuel on the return flight. At 10,000 feet, in accordance with their prearranged plan, the two pilots signaled to each other that everything was working.

But the brown haze threatened to upset their calculations. It blotted out the landmarks they had hoped to navigate by and forced them to fly by compass. The ground checkpoint where the survey cameras were to start mapping was invisible in the murk, though Clydesdale climbed more slowly than he had intended in a vain effort to spot it. Even more worrisome, the haze made it impossible to judge the planes' rate of drift in the west-to-east crosswind. The plan was to climb steadily to a point several thousand feet above the windward side of the summit and thus avoid the downdrafts that were more likely on the lee side, but the plan did not allow for the intrusive haze.

At 19,000 feet the fliers suddenly popped through the top of the haze and saw its level roof beneath them. To McIntyre "it appeared as though we peeped over the edge of an enormous round tabletop of brown ground glass." Now they could see the awesome mountains ahead, clustered in a semicircle perhaps 50 miles away and shining in the crystalline air. From this close they looked gigantic, even grander than the fliers had imagined. Beyond Everest a battalion of peaks marched north and west until they nudged the horizon several hundred miles away; the angle caused some of them to appear to soar higher

Riding at the head of a train of richly caparisoned elephants, a local potentate—curious to observe the latest in flying machines—makes a stately entrance at the Everest expedition's airfield near the foothills of the Himalayas.

than Everest. The layer of haze above the snow line made the mountains seem detached, a world apart—"an eerie land," Clydesdale wrote, "floating in a drab sea somewhere between earth and sky."

As they plotted their position they could now add up how much the haze had cost them. Blacker found that they had drifted 18 degrees off their course, which indicated a stronger westerly wind than the 58 miles an hour that had been reported. The telltale plume they saw streaming from the summit of Everest confirmed this; its tail reached nearly halfway to Makalu, 12 miles east of Everest.

The wind had blown them too far to the east. To arrive over the crest on the windward side they would now have to crab into the wind on a northwesterly heading, bucking the gusts while trying to climb 14,000 feet in 50 miles. It soon became clear that they could not do it; they had counted on having 4,000 feet of altitude above Everest's peak, but now they would be lucky to have 1,000. The violent wind was also pushing them inexorably in the direction of the lee side and the downdrafts.

Blacker, manning the cameras in the cabin of the *Houston-Westland,* switched on the electricity and felt his flight suit begin to warm as they climbed past 20,000 and then 25,000 feet. At intervals he poked his head out of the top of his compartment and snapped photographs in the frigid air. Clydesdale, sitting in his open cockpit, was pleased by the way his engine responded but worried about the oxygen supply. He reduced the flow in order to conserve it, but Blacker, whose job required more exertion and therefore more oxygen than the pilot needed, passed him an urgent note asking for more flow. Then Clydesdale's own vision began to darken and his feet to cramp and he turned the valve back up, feeling relief immediately. He noticed that the peaks did not seem to be getting any closer—an illusion he attributed to their bulk. McIntyre, in the second plane, was having trouble maintaining his climbing angle. He guessed that the reason was his heavier load—Bonnett's movie cameras.

Within minutes both planes were closing on Lhotse, the peak just southeast of Everest. Makalu was to their right and Everest dead ahead. They were still fighting for altitude, but McIntyre seemed to be losing the battle. Clydesdale was edging close to 31,000 feet, with McIntyre well below him. And both of them were about to be bushwhacked.

Clydesdale felt it first. In the space of a few seconds the downdraft dropped his plane 2,000 feet. "Down we went irresistibly in this current, although the engine throttle was wide open and the machine still at its maximum climbing angle." Now he was only a few hundred feet higher than the summit of Everest and fighting hard to maintain his altitude. He ignored the instrument panel and flew by sight, eyeballing Lhotse as it rushed toward him and then receded, to his enormous relief, behind the plane's tail and perhaps 50 feet below it. A few seconds later he flew through the ice cloud that forms Everest's plume and felt "a moderately hefty bump." Immediately after this an updraft seized the plane and flung it upward as fast as it had fallen only moments earlier. "We now rose directly over the summit of Everest," he reported coolly, "and cleared it comparatively comfortably by about 500 feet."

From Blacker's vantage point—an open trap door in the plane's floor—the margin of safety seemed even narrower. The "curved chisel-like summit" flashed by so close that he felt he could almost lean out and touch it. "The crest came up to meet me as I crouched peering through the floor," he said, "and I almost wondered whether the tail skid would strike the summit." Gasping for breath, he scrambled to his feet and thrust head and shoulders into the slip stream to photograph what he thought of as "nature's last terrestrial secret."

McIntyre and Bonnett were waging an even more desperate struggle in the Wallace. Caught by the downdraft while still beneath the level of the highest crests, they were hurled down below the ridge connecting Everest and Makalu and found themselves walled in on three sides. "There was plenty of air space behind us," McIntyre recalled afterward, "yet it was impossible to turn back. A turn to the left meant going back into the down-current and the peaks below; a turn downwind to the right would have taken us almost instantly into Makalu at 200 miles an hour. There was nothing we could do but climb straight ahead and hope to clear the lowest point in the barrier range."

McIntyre flew toward the ridge and into the wind, unsure if he could get the plane over. An updraft a few yards short of the barrier lifted him just enough to clear the top of the ridge. "Then started a grim fight for height," he continued. "We had to turn very carefully toward Everest and then back over the ridge again with the little height that we had gained and face the same fight over again." Each time he turned toward Everest he risked being seized once more by the downdraft—"it was very much like a nightmare"—but he continued to cross and recross the ridge, ascending slightly with each crossing. He tried to memorize the precise location of the invisible down current by using terrain features to mark what he thought were its borders. "Three times we had to repeat this performance, gaining a little height each time, until we reckoned we had sufficient height to venture round the north side and over the top of Everest."

Bonnett had been calmly shooting pictures from an open hatch as McIntyre maneuvered the plane back and forth, but as they neared the crest he went down into the cabin to reload his cameras. As he worked he inadvertently stepped on the tube carrying his oxygen and broke it. Rapidly losing consciousness, he managed to find the rupture and tried without success to stop the leak by wrapping a handkerchief tightly around the break. He fell to the floor when he tried to climb through the open hatch to resume shooting. McIntyre saw him slip out of sight and realized that something was wrong but was powerless to help.

Clydesdale had meanwhile headed into the teeth of the wind after crossing the summit in hopes of getting a picture of the mountain's unknown west face, but the persistent westerly gale forced him to swing around to the northeast. He was relieved to see McIntyre, still inching upward toward his first pass over the crest, fly by him going the other way; they had lost contact with each other when they hit the downdraft. McIntyre crept over the top—"a tiny platform that appeared to have standing room for about four people"—while Clydesdale circled the northeast ridge. Blacker estimated that they were in the vicinity of the summit for about 15 minutes before the two planes, once again flying in tandem, turned for home.

McIntyre, still uncertain whether Bonnett was alive or dead, was suddenly confronted with another emergency. He tried to catch a glimpse of Bonnett and felt a cold stab of pain on his face: The nosepiece on his oxygen mask had come off when he turned his head. He saw the piece, which contained his breathing apparatus, lying on his knee. Grabbing it with a gloved hand, he clumsily tried to reattach it to the mask but could not get it in place. He decided to hold it to his face until they were low enough that he did not need it. For the next half hour he held the nosepiece in one hand while flying the plane with the other. By that time he had descended to 16,000 feet and was once again in the haze, but he could get by without oxygen. After losing another 8,000 feet of altitude he was aware of a movement behind him and saw Bonnett, green-faced and shaken but otherwise unharmed, struggling to his feet. The crisis was past.

Twenty more minutes brought them back to the midday heat of Lalbalu. It was April 3, 1933. The aerial conquest of the world's highest mountain had taken just over three hours.

The euphoric reaction back home in England—"it is almost like exploring the rainbow," the London *Times* crowed, "to have traveled direct to that immense, remote, tethered cloud"—was dampened only slightly by the fusty complaints of some that Everest could only be truly conquered by mountaineers, a feat that would not be achieved for 20 more years. But the jubilation among the crew at Purnea was quickly cut short by the discovery that they had failed in their main scientific objective: The haze had prevented them from compiling an accurate sequence of overlapping film strips for the mapmakers. Fellowes, anxious to make sure that the survey cameras were working properly, took off the next day to test them on a flight over Kanchenjunga, an only slightly less imposing peak 70 miles southeast of Everest. The commodore was disappointed to find the summit hidden by clouds; the cameras, however, performed flawlessly.

Fellowes and his crew had known from the outset that a second flight over Everest might be necessary to complete their survey; they now considered it imperative. But the chilling accounts of the first flight that had appeared in English newspapers had tempered the patriotic ardor of their backers. A telegram arrived from Lady Houston, advising them gently to "be content. Do not tempt the evil spirits of the mountain to bring disaster." The firm that had insured the expedition announced that its coverage did not extend to another Everest flight. After several days of long-distance bickering the party

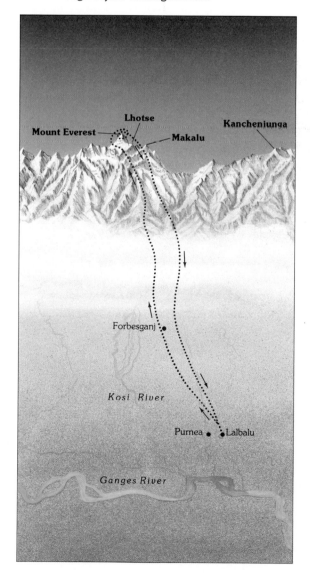

This diagram traces the first 320-mile round-trip flight by Lord Clydesdale and Flight Lieutenant McIntyre from Lalbalu airfield in India to 29,028-foot-high Mount Everest, and home again. The Himalayan foothills were blanketed by a 10,000-foot-high dust cloud that the explorers in their Westland biplanes had to climb through before cresting Everest.

Lhotse

Mount Everest —

Makalu

Kanchenjunga

Forbesganj

Kosi River

Purnea   Lalbalu

Ganges River

was officially ordered to return home. Fellowes promised to obey.

But Clydesdale, McIntyre and Blacker were unwilling to let it go at that. Blacker's reaction was characteristically stiff-upper-lip. To have quit at this point, he wrote later, "would have been shameful beyond words, because there was no reason against a second flight except the personal risk." The rebels decided to go anyway; if this was insubordination—and it was—they would make the most of it.

Fellowes, as the leader, would have to be circumvented. The pilots asked him for permission to make a special flight so that film maker Geoffrey Barkas could get some needed shots of the mountains. Fellowes agreed, on condition that the planes were never out of emergency landing range of the flatlands: If the engine failed, they had to be close enough to glide to a landing. Fortunately for the plotters, Fellowes then fell ill and, bedridden, was unable to give them his full attention. Clydesdale and McIntyre quietly charted a new course. The low-altitude winds over the plain, they had discovered, normally blew from the east. By flying low until they reached the mountains they could take advantage of these wind currents before climbing sharply to pick up the high-country westerlies. They could then approach Everest from the west and avoid the downdrafts.

When Fellowes appeared to be recovering, on April 18, they knew that they had to act fast. The weather report on the 19th showed a wind velocity of 88 miles an hour at 24,000 feet—stronger winds than they had met on the first flight. It was also cloudy over the field. But for the conspirators it was now or never.

With Clydesdale again flying in the lead, the two Westlands cruised beneath the clouds at 2,000 feet for the first 50 miles and then climbed through a gap in the overcast, emerging on top of the fleece at 18,000 feet. This time the view on high was even better; the bright white of clouds and ice seemed to deepen the blue of the sky. Clydesdale, reluctant to switch on their precious oxygen until he was sure they could achieve their goal, finally opened the valves at 21,000 feet.

The plume tailing off from the top of Everest—it was longer than the six-mile streak they had seen on their first flight—told them that the wind was indeed stronger than it had been before; they estimated the wind speed at 120 miles per hour. Despite the fact that they had taken a more westerly course, both pilots were again being shoved toward the lee side of the peak. They approached the unexplored southern flanks, their prime photographic target, at 31,000 feet and began clicking off camera exposures at 15-second intervals. Blacker adjusted the camera to allow for the strong drift, which seemed to Clydesdale to be pushing them sideways faster than they were going forward.

Both planes climbed to 34,000 feet. Clydesdale veered to the east before he reached Everest and hurtled off toward Makalu with the wind now at his back, but McIntyre wanted another look at the highest crest. The summit "appeared to be almost underneath us but refused to get right beneath," he said. "After what seemed an interminable time it

Lord Clydesdale's P.V.3, seen from the other Westland, nears Everest at 32,000 feet. The ice plume blowing from the peak signaled fierce winds.

disappeared below the nose of the aircraft." A few seconds later the plane was rocked by the ferocious turbulence that always swirls above a mountain's crown. It seemed to McIntyre as if they "were flying low over an explosive factory as it blew up." A hasty check revealed that the Westland had withstood the blast without damage; every wire was still taut. McIntyre was now content to bank toward Makalu and follow Clydesdale back to the field.

With the conclusion of this flight, described by the London *Times* as "a piece of magnificent insubordination," the remarkable work of the British Mount Everest expedition of 1933 was completed. Their secret and defiant mission had produced precisely the results they had hoped for, a clear sequence of survey pictures depicting a landscape that no one had viewed before. Geographers could now add several new pieces to their portrait of Everest, among them two previously unknown glaciers and a glacial lake at 18,000 feet; the Scotsman McIntyre wanted to call it Loch Everest. The photographs and movies that the observers had suffered so to produce still rank with the most spectacular mountain views ever captured on film.

As for the pilots, a journalist accompanying the expedition called their performance "as fine a piece of cool and careful flying in unfamiliar and dangerous circumstances as their generation produced." But like many other aviators, the conquerors of Mount Everest became embarrassed when they heard words like that. Sometimes the extremes of aeronautical modesty approached the ludicrous: "I would like to say that this flight was really nothing," Clydesdale declared soon after he returned home to Scotland. "It was very much like performing an ordinary Royal Air Force duty."

The brilliant triumph of the British Mount Everest expedition was the climactic achievement of the great age of aerial exploration, an era that had begun with Roald Amundsen's ill-starred North Pole flight. Amundsen, Ellsworth, Byrd, Wilkins, Cobham, Mittelholzer, Clydesdale—one by one the ever-questing explorers had marked out their goals on the map and gone on to achieve them. Beckoned onward by a dynamic technology, the intrepid aviators had rolled back the curtains concealing the last of the earth's great geographic mysteries in a single 10-year span. Polar ice fields, matted jungles and cloud-piercing mountains had been seen, photographed, charted and explained for the first time.

But the dream of the explorer—the dream of discovery—would persist. The first generation of aerial explorers would be succeeded by others who would ride the hurtling technology of flight to still more frontiers of science and knowledge. They would look more closely at the wonders that the first explorers had uncovered and they would find new areas—archeology is only one example—where the airplane could be a vehicle of discovery. Eventually the imagination of the aerial explorers would carry them beyond the earth to the realm of the deepest and most abiding mysteries of all—outer space. ⌇

Land of lost horizons

Flying high above the Peruvian Andes in 1928, American aerial photographer George Johnson came upon a string of villages nestled deep in a magnificent gorge known as the Colca Valley. The villages were neatly laid out in colonial Spanish style, with well-tilled terraces of crops. But the villages appeared on no maps, and Johnson's photographs stirred a sensation in Lima, where no one seemed to know anything about the "lost" villages of Colca.

Johnson was so fascinated that in 1931 he and another American, Robert Shippee, returned to visit the Colca Valley and launch an aerial survey of all of Peru in hopes of turning up other hidden wonders. They confirmed that the people within the confines of the valley were the remnants of a much larger Indian population that had gradually lost touch, until now the villagers were virtually cut off from civilization. Johnson and Shippee went on to spend eight months exploring the country. From their Bellanca monoplanes *Lima* and *Washington,* they photographed spectacular deserts, volcanoes, and inaccessible valleys and canyons. But their most fascinating pictures were of ruins of ancient Indian civilizations, among them a previously unrecorded giant stone wall the pilots followed over the mountains for 40 miles before fog forced them back. "It is still hard for us to believe," Shippee wrote later, "that we have actually made a new discovery of such importance."

Robert Shippee (above, left) and George Johnson show off the pet they picked up in the Colca Valley. Their plane, the first ever to land there, was welcomed by banner-waving Indians

A band of curious pockmarks, perhaps excavated graves or depressions left from pre-Columbian surface mining, stipples a hillside in southern Peru. Although intrigued by the holes, the explorers were unable to investigate further because the rocky terrain prevented them from landing.

Oddly shaped sand dunes formed by constantly blowing winds dot the desert beneath the Lima in this photograph taken from the Washington

Extinct volcanic cones and great fields of hardened lava mark the desert not far from the Colca Valley. Shippee and Johnson camped inside the 350-foot-wide cone in the foreground.

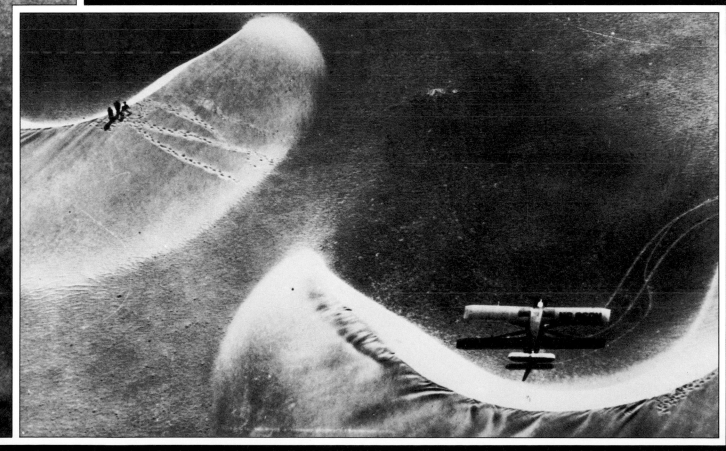

Sheltered by a 30-foot-high dune, the Lima awaits the return of its crew. Such dunes advanced 60 feet a year.

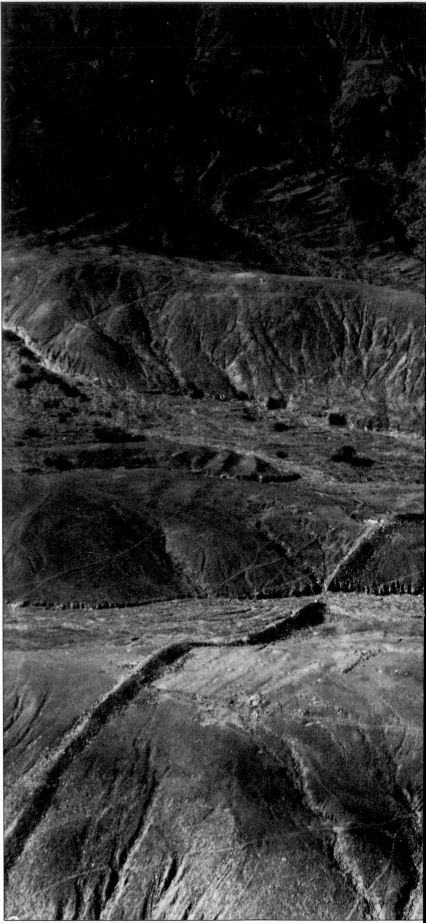

Peru's Great Wall, Shippee and Johnson's most spectacular aerial discovery, climbs the Andean foothills near the ancient Chimú capital of Chan-Chan. In the immediate foreground are the ruins of a fortress. Like the 15-foot-high wall, this fort and 13 others along its length probably offered the Chimú protection against Inca invaders.

Acknowledgments

The index for this book was prepared by Gale Linck Partoyan. For their help in the preparation of this volume, the editors thank: **In Australia:** South Australia—Dr. F. Jacka, Director, Mawson Institute of Antarctic Research, University of Adelaide. **In Canada:** Ontario—Louise Guay-Bourassa, Public Archives of Canada, National Photography Collection. **In the Federal Republic of Germany:** Berlin (West)—Wolfgang Streubel, Ullstein Bilderdienst; Cologne—Werner Bittner, Marga Hühnerback, Deutsche Lufthansa; Mainz-Finthen—Karl Ries; Munich—Herbert Studtrucker, Deutsches Museum. **In France:** Paris—Gérard Baschet, Éditions de l'Illustration; Colonel Edmond Petit, Curator, Musée Air-France; Georges Delaleau, Général Pierre Lissarague, Director, Jean-Yves Lorent, Général Roger de Ruffray, Deputy-Director, Colonel Pierre Willefert, Curator, Musée de l'Air. **In the German Democratic Republic:** Berlin (East)—Hannes Quaschinsky, ADN-Zentralbild. **In Great Britain:** Cambridge—Professor J.K.S. St. Joseph; Dorset—T. W. Brooks-Smith, Michael Cobham, Christopher Farquharson-Roberts, Flight Refuelling Ltd.; Essex—A. J. Jackson; Hatfield—John Scott, British Aerospace; London—John Bagley, Science Museum; T. Betts, the National Monuments Record; R. W. Mack, Royal Air Force Museum; Arnold Nayler, Royal Aeronautical Society; Marjorie Willis, BBC Hulton Picture Library. **In Italy:** Rome—Contessa Maria Fede Caproni, Museo Aeronautico Caproni di Taliedo. **In the Union of Soviet Socialist Republics:** Moscow—E. Riabko-Minkin. **In the United States:** Alaska—Renee Blahuta, University of Alaska Library; Connecticut—Judith Schiff, Yale Sterling Library, Manuscript and Archives Division; Washington, D.C.—Deane Boyden, Defense Mapping Agency; Dr. Philip K. Lundeberg, Curator, Division of Naval History, Museum of American History, the Smithsonian Institution; Dr. Franklin W. Burch, Chief, Sharon Gibbs, Archives Technician, Alison Wilson, Archives Technician, Scientific, Economic and Natural Resources Branch, National Archives; Paul Sampson, Chief of the News Service, National Geographic Society; Kansas—Barbara Henshall, Curator, the Martin & Osa Johnson Safari Museum; Maryland—Henry Beville; Jaime Quintero; Michigan—David Crippen, Reference Archivist, Archives and Research Library, Henry Ford Museum and Greenfield Village; New York—Jesse Davidson; William K. Kaiser, Curator, Cradle of Aviation Museum; Dr. Douglas McManis, American Geographic Society; Ohio—Dr. David Bromwich, Polar Studies Institute, Ohio State University; Pennsylvania—Marley Stevens Ross, President, Winston Ross, Vice President, Wilkins Memorial Foundation; Virginia—Louis S. Casey; Bill Hezlep; Washington—Lillian Frizell; Steve Small, *The Vancouver Columbian;* Robert W. Stevens; Wisconsin—Ellen Murphy, Cataloguer/Reference Librarian, American Geographical Society Collection, University of Wisconsin-Milwaukee.

Bibliography

Books
Amundsen, Roald:
    My Polar Flight. London: Hutchinson & Co., 1925.
    Roald Amundsen—My Life as an Explorer. Doubleday, Page & Company, 1927.
Archbold, Richard, and A. L. Rand, *New Guinea Expedition: Fly River Area, 1936-1937.* Robert M. McBride and Co., 1940.
Baidukov, George, *Over the North Pole.* Transl. by Jessica Smith. Harcourt, Brace and Co., 1938.
Balchen, Bernt, *Come North with Me.* E. P. Dutton & Co., Inc., 1958.
Bennett, Cora L., *Floyd Bennett.* William Farquhar Payson, 1932.
Bertrand, Kenneth J., *Americans in Antarctica, 1775-1948.* American Geographical Society, 1971.
Byrd, Richard Evelyn, *Little America: Aerial Exploration in the Antarctic: The Flight to the South Pole.* G. P. Putnam's Sons, 1930.
Carlson, William S., *Lifelines through the Arctic.* Duell, Sloan and Pearce, 1962.
Clarke, Basil, *Polar Flight.* London: Ian Allan Ltd., 1964.
Cobham, Alan J.:
    My Flight to the Cape and Back. London: A. & C. Black, Ltd., 1926.
    A Time to Fly. London: Shepheard-Walwyn, 1978.
Deuel, Leo, *Flights into Yesterday: The Story of Aerial Archaeology.* St. Martin's Press, 1969.
Douglas-Hamilton, Douglas, Marquis of Douglas and Clydesdale, and D. F. M'Intyre, *The Pilots' Book of Everest.* London: William Hodge & Company, Limited, 1936.
Ellsworth, Lincoln, *Beyond Horizons.* Doubleday, Doran & Company, Inc., 1938.

Fellowes, Air-Commodore P.F.M., Squadron Leader the Marquis of Douglas and Clydesdale, L. V. Stewart Blacker and Colonel P. T. Etherton, *First over Everest! The Houston-Mount Everest Expedition, 1933.* Robert M. McBride & Company, 1934.
Glines, Lt. Col. C. V., ed., *Polar Aviation.* Franklin Watts, Inc., 1964.
Grierson, John:
    Challenge to the Poles: Highlights of Arctic and Antarctic Aviation. London: G. T. Foulis & Co. Ltd., 1964.
    Sir Hubert Wilkins, Enigma of Exploration. London: Robert Hale Limited, 1960.
Hitchins, Captain H. L., and Commander W. E. May, *From Lodestone to Gyro-Compass.* London: Hutchinson's Scientific and Technical Publications, 1952.
Hoyt, Edwin P., *The Last Explorer: The Adventures of Admiral Byrd.* The John Day Company, 1968.
Joerg, W.L.G.:
    Polar Exploration since the Introduction of Flying. American Geographical Society, 1930.
    The Work of the Byrd Antarctic Expedition 1928-1930. American Geographical Society, 1930.
Johnson, Osa, *I Married Adventure: The Lives and Adventures of Martin and Osa Johnson.* J. B. Lippincott Company, 1940.
Light, Richard Upjohn, *Focus on Africa.* American Geographical Society, 1944.
Lindbergh, Anne Morrow, *North to the Orient.* Harcourt, Brace and Company, 1935.
Mittelholzer, Walter, *Flying Adventures.* London: Blackie & Son Limited, 1936.
Montague, Richard, *Oceans, Poles and Airmen: The First Flights over Wide Waters and Desolate Ice.* Random House, 1971.
Nobile, Umberto, *My Polar Flights: An Account of the Voyages of the Airships Italia and Norge.* Transl. by Frances Fleetwood. London: Frederick Muller Limited, 1961.
Thomas, Lowell, *Sir Hubert Wilkins: His World of Adventure.* McGraw-Hill, 1961.
Weems, P.V.H., *Air Navigation.* McGraw-Hill, 1938.
Wilkins, Captain George H., *Flying the Arctic.* G. P. Putnam's Sons, 1928.

Periodicals
Archbold, Richard, "Unknown New Guinea." *The National Geographic Magazine,* March 1941.
Brandes, E. W., "Into Primeval Papua by Seaplane." *The National Geographic Magazine,* September 1929.
Byrd, Richard E.:
    "The First Flight to the North Pole." *The National Geographic Magazine,* September 1926.
    "Straight to the North Pole!" *The New York Times Magazine,* June 20, 1926.
De Pinedo, Comdr. Francesco, "By Seaplane to Six Continents." *The National Geographic Magazine,* September 1928.
Hinton, Walter, "Flying over the Brazilian Jungles." *The World's Work,* October 1925.
Rabot, Charles, "The Norwegians in Spitsbergen." *The Geographical Review,* October-November 1919.
Stefansson, Vilhjalmur, "The Arctic as an Air Route of the Future." *The National Geographic Magazine,* August 1922.
Wilkins, Sir Hubert:
    "Our Search for the Lost Aviators." *The National Geographic Magazine,* August 1938.
    "The Wilkins-Hearst Antarctic Expedition, 1928-1929." *The Geographical Review,* July 1929.

Picture credits

Credits from left to right are separated by semicolons, from top to bottom by dashes.
Endpaper (and cover detail, regular edition): Painting by Paul Lengellé. 7: Lomen Family Collection 72-71-28, Archives, University of Alaska, Fairbanks. 8: Library of Congress. 9: UPI. 10: National Air and Space Museum, Smithsonian Institution (No. 82-11338). 11: Ullstein Bilderdienst, Berlin (West). 12: The Martin & Osa Johnson Safari Museum. 13: The Bettmann Archive. 14: Popperfoto, London. 15: ADN-Zentralbild, Berlin (DDR). 16: Lomen Family Collection 72-71-126, Archives, University of Alaska, Fairbanks. 17-19: Library of Congress. 23: Library of Congress—From *The Aerial Age,* by Walter Wellman © 1911 A. R. Keller. 25: Courtesy Norsk Teknisk Museum, Oslo. 27: Map by Bill Hezlep. 28, 29: From the American Geographical Society, Collection of the University of Milwaukee-Wisconsin. 30: Norsk Teknisk Museum, Oslo. 31: From *Air Pioneering in the Arctic,* by Roald Amundsen and Lincoln Ellsworth, published by National Americana Society, N.Y., 1929. 33: Library of Congress. 35: National Air and Space Museum, Smithsonian Institution (No. 82-11341). 36, 37: Norsk Teknisk Museum, Oslo. 38: From *Air Pioneering in the Arctic,* by Roald Amundsen and

Lincoln Ellsworth, published by National Americana Society, N.Y., 1929. 39: Library of Congress. 41: Charles Bunnell Collection, Archives, University of Alaska, Fairbanks. 45: Wide World, courtesy Wilkins Memorial Foundation; courtesy Wilkins Memorial Foundation. 46-55: Courtesy American Geographical Society. 56, 57: FPG. 59, 60: *The New York Times.* 62: Ullstein Bilderdienst, Berlin (West). 65: Map by Bill Hezlep. 66: UPI. 68: Library of Congress. 70: Ralph Vincent, courtesy Jim Vincent. 71-75: E. Riabko-Minkin and VAAP, Moscow. 76, 77: National Archives (No. 410-36). 79: National Library of Australia, Canberra. 80: Map by Bill Hezlep. 82: Courtesy the American Museum of Natural History. 83-88: National Archives (Nos. 306-NT-547c-15, RG 200, RG 401/73, RG 401/4, 306-NT-548-61). 89: © Byrd Antarctic Expedition, by permission of Richard Byrd III; National Archives(2) (Nos. RG 401/4, RG 401/59). 91-99: National Archives (Nos. 306-NT-548-1, 306-NT-548A-7, 306-NT-548-7, 401-36, 401/36 Ellsworth). 101: Courtesy American Geographical Society. 102-107: National Archives (Nos. 306-NT-548-43, RG 200 BAE I, RG 200(3)). 108, 109: National Air and Space Museum, Smithsonian Institution (No. 76-17139). 110, 111: National Archives (No. 306-

NT-116866). 113: *Flight International,* courtesy British Aerospace, Hatfield, England. 115: Flight Refuelling, Ltd., Wimborne, Dorset, England—Brian Thomas, Brighton, England. 116, 117: Flight Refuelling, Ltd., Wimborne, Dorset, England. 119: Map by Bill Hezlep. 120, 122: UPI. 124-127: National Archives (Nos. 306-NT-554-1, 306-NT-558-1, 306-NT-558-5). 129: Map by Bill Hezlep. 132: Gwynn-Jones Collection. 134, 135: Courtesy the American Museum of Natural History. 136-143: Drawings by John Batchelor. 144, 145: © *The Times,* London. 146: Giancarlo Costa, courtesy *La Tribuna Illustrata,* Milan. 148, 149: Swissair Vermessungen, Zurich. 152: From the American Geographical Society, Collection of the University of Wisconsin-Milwaukee. 154-157: © *The Times,* London. 161: Art by Jaime Quintero. 162, 163: © *The Times,* London. 164, 165: National Archives (No. 306-NT-550-6); from the American Geographical Society, Collection of the University of Wisconsin-Milwaukee. 166, 167: National Archives (No. 306 NT-550-4); Courtesy the American Museum of Natural History. 168, 169: National Archives (Nos. 306-NT-115832, 306-NT-115836, 306-NT-115834). 170, 171: Courtesy the American Museum of Natural History.

Index